"BY THE HANDS OF WISE MEN"

"BY THE HANDS OF WISE MEN"

ESSAYS ON THE U.S. CONSTITUTION

Ray C. Hillam, editor

Brigham Young University Press

Library of Congress Cataloging in Publication Data
Main entry under title:

"By the hands of wise men."

Includes index.
1. United States—Constitutional law—Moral and
religious aspects—Addresses, essays, lectures.
2. Mormons and Mormonism—Doctrinal and controversial
works—Addresses, essays, lectures.   I. Hillam, Ray C.
KF4550.A2B9   342'.73   79-13702
ISBN 0-8425-1647-6

International Standard Book Number: 0-8425-1647-6
Brigham Young University Press, Provo, Utah 84602
© 1979 by Brigham Young University Press. All rights reserved
Printed in the United States of America
7/79 3Mp 37556

Our forefathers left us a free government which is a miracle of faith—strong, durable, marvelously workable. Yet it can remain so only as long as we understand it, believe in it, devote ourselves to it, and when necessary, fight for it.

President Ezra Taft Benson
Quorum of the Twelve Apostles
June 2, 1978

Contents

"By the Hands of Wise Men": Essays on the U.S. Constitution

THIS BOOK IS AN OUTGROWTH of a symposium sponsored by the College of Social Sciences in commemoration of the centennial of Brigham Young University. The purpose of the symposium was twofold: to instill confidence in the American constitutional system and to provide a forum for an exchange of ideas by constitutional scholars. The essays and lectures in this volume have the same purpose, but they have been rewritten specifically for the undergraduate student.

Mormons have a unique view of the American Constitution. They have been taught in their formative years that it is an inspired document established "by the hands of wise men." They have been taught from the pulpit, in Sunday School classes, and in Mormon homes. This concept is found in Mormon literature, and most importantly it is specifically discussed in the Doctrine and Covenants (latter-day revelation) and by General Authorities in the conferences of the Church. Almost all discussions, however, are general and do not refer to specific details. Certain questions are left unanswered.

Do all Mormons fully understand and appreciate the importance of constitutional government? Do they comprehend the interaction of the Founding Fathers and the will of God in this matter? Why is the Constitution and its preservation important to the Mormons? And finally, what are the citizenship responsibilities of Mormons who live under the American constitutional system? The essays and lectures in this volume are addressed to these and similar questions.

The contributors to this volume have devoted much of their academic and professional careers to studying, writing, and teaching about the American Constitution. They have been educated or trained in the disciplines of history, economics, law, philosophy, and political science; and all are students of the scriptures and have served in a wide range of ecclesiastical roles for The Church of Jesus Christ of Latter-day Saints. Their essays combine scholarship and the special language of the Latter-day Saint faith, making this a unique and useful supplement to the study of constitutional government.

It is hoped that the reader, picking and choosing from the variety offered, will come from the experience of reading these essays better informed about the Latter-day Saint view of the U.S. Constitution and with a stronger commitment to those "just and holy principles" found in the American constitutional system.

I appreciate the encouragement of many colleagues who feel that these essays should be in print and available to our students. I also appreciate the sponsorship of the Social Science Centennial Symposium which led to the preparation of this volume.

Ray C. Hillam
May 1979

"BY THE HANDS
OF WISE MEN"

The Doctrine of an Inspired Constitution *

Noel B. Reynolds, associate professor of political philosophy, says that the American Constitution is an inspired document. Because of increased secularization in America, Reynolds says Mormons now find themselves almost alone in their belief that God played a fundamental role in the founding of their nation. Unlike most Americans, Mormons believe that the Constitution was inspired by God. Reynolds argues that historical facts are compatible with the teaching that the Constitution was inspired by God. The argument details several cultural developments in eighteenth-century America which uniquely prepared the Americans for the formulation and successful implementation of a constitution of liberty. He likens this historical development to the divine inspiration exemplified in various Church programs which developed through experimentation (i.e., welfare programs). Reynolds emphasizes the central importance of the rule of law in the Constitution as the prime connecting link with political principles sanctioned in scripture. Rule of law is essential, he says, to a free society. He concludes that our liberty and the preservation of inspired constitutional principles is dependent upon morality and a certain measure of public virtue. He then echoes the exhortations of both ancient and modern prophets who promised the people that their free government would endure only if they were righteous and served the God of the land.

Professor Reynolds has a Ph.D. from the Department of Government at Harvard University. He has served as chairman of the Department of Philosophy at Brigham Young University and has completed one year of postdoctoral study as a Fellow in Law and Philosophy at the Harvard School of Law. He is currently on the faculty of the Department of Government at Brigham Young University.

*Reprinted from *Brigham Young University Studies* (Spring 1976) by permission of the author and publisher; copyright 1976 by Brigham Young University Press.

1

EIGHTEENTH- AND NINETEENTH-CENTURY Americans very commonly assumed that the guiding hand of God was largely responsible for the founding of their new nation, that God had "called forth certain hardy souls from the old and privilege-ridden nations," and that he "had carried these precious few to a new world and presented them and their descendants with an environment ideally suited to the development of a free society."[1] Although this Puritan view "had its classic expression during the Revolution and constitutional period, . . . [it] has appeared repeatedly in the course of American history."[2]

The echoes of this providential view of America's origins sounded down through the nineteenth century and were even heard in the writings of notable historians.[3] But in the twentieth century, both professional historians and Americans generally have been overtaken by secularization. As our contemporaries look back on the events of those formative years, they fail to discern the guiding hand of God. They satisfy themselves with the sophisticated assurance that the providential views of our ancestors were either rhetoric or mythology.[4] In the twentieth century, we Mormons find ourselves almost alone in our belief that God did play a fundamental role in the founding of our nation, and that the American Constitution was inspired by him.[5]

In the Church today, we speak frequently and loosely of our view that the Constitution was inspired. We can cite numerous clear statements by our prophets which elaborate this idea. In 1833, Joseph Smith recorded the scriptural statement that the Lord "established the Constitution of this land, by the hands of wise men whom [He] raised up unto this very purpose" (D&C 101:80).[6] In an official declaration of Church belief, the First Presidency recently affirmed that

> we believe that the Constitution of the United States was divinely inspired, that it was produced by "wise men" whom God raised up for this "very purpose," and that the principles embodied in the Constitution are so fundamental and important that, if possible, they should be extended "for the rights and protection" of all mankind.[7]

The commitment of these Church leaders to the view that God was integrally involved in the formulation of the Constitution is unequivocal. Yet this may seem problematic for those Latter-day Saints who have grown up with the "demythologizing" accounts of Charles Beard and other progressivist historians who have insisted on explaining the Constitution primarily as a political compromise between competing economic interests.[8] Because of the pervasive influence of these secular views in modern histories and textbooks, most Americans may not realize that over the past decades the major arguments of the old progressivist school have been significantly qualified by careful researchers.[9]

The historical facts are in every way compatible with the teaching that the Constitution was inspired by God. The question of inspiration should not focus exclusively on a few men in Independence Hall in that hot summer of 1787, but also on the gathering together of a people with beliefs conducive to forming a new, free republic. Inspiration can also operate in a diffused manner in the struggle of faithful men to find long-range solutions to real problems, as is illustrated by many developments in Church practice. A confirmation of this kind of inspiration in the Constitution can be found in the recognition that the central principles of rule of law, which the drafters built into the Constitution, are essentially identical to those "just and holy principles" which, according to the scripture, justify the Constitution in the eyes of the Lord.

Wise Men Raised Up for This Very Purpose

The revelation recorded by Joseph Smith calls our attention directly to those "wise men" that God "raised up" to establish the Constitution. Many commentators have been impressed by the high character and remarkable political wisdom of the leading American statesmen of the constitutional period. The prominent historian, Henry Steele Commager, wrote:

> Yet who can doubt that in the last quarter of the eighteenth century it was the New World—not democracy by our standards but certainly democracy by European—that provided the most impressive spectacle of leadership, rather than the nations of the Old World? Who can doubt, for example, that in the crisis of 1774–1783, the American colonies and states enjoyed far more competent leadership than the British Empire?
>
> The situation is too familiar to rehearse. In the last quarter of the century the new United States—a nation with a white population of less than three million, without a single major city, and wholly lacking in those institutions of organized society or civilization so familiar in Europe—boasted a galaxy of leaders who were quite literally incomparable: Franklin, Washington, Jefferson, Hamilton, John Adams, Samuel Adams, John Jay, James Wilson, George Mason, Benjamin Rush, James Madison, and a dozen others scarcely less distinguished.
>
> What explains this remarkable outpouring of political leadership, this fertility in the production of statesmen—a fertility unmatched since that day? Was it an historical accident? Was it a peculiar response to the time or the place, or to a combination of the two? Or was it a product of

conditions and attitudes that were cultivated and directed to calculated ends, and that can be if not re-created at least paralleled in our time?[10]

Such statements testify to the striking political wisdom and leadership of American statesmen in the eighteenth century. What is not as often recognized is that the American people themselves were a remarkable group. Historians have generally acknowledged the unusual political literacy of the eighteenth-century Americans, but because of their presumed lack of formal education, this high political literacy has often been discounted by the assumption that their beliefs were largely naive and ideological. Fortunately, careful historical inquiry into the political discourses of eighteenth-century America has illuminated anew the depths at which the political wisdom of the Founding Fathers ran simultaneously through the general populace.

Bernard Bailyn has opened our eyes to the flood of political tracts and treatises that washed across pre-Revolutionary America.[11] The sustained success of these publications testifies that people were buying and reading them. A contemporary observer remarked that in Massachusetts,

> knowledge, at least in its first degrees, is extensively diffused. Not a house is to be found in the most remote corners of the country where a newspaper is not read; and there are few townships which do not possess a little library formed and supported by subscription.[12]

Although it is true that formal education was beyond the means of large numbers of Americans, the picture emerging today suggests that they were a surprisingly literate people and that their intelligent and informed interest in public affairs was extraordinary among eighteenth-century societies.[13]

As significant as the political literacy of the people was, the strong spiritual foundations of colonial America were even more important. The major thrust of American settlement came from English Puritans, and this Puritanism "provided the moral and religious background of fully 75 per cent of the people"[14] even as late as 1776. Transplanted to the free soil of America, English Puritanism thrived and flourished; the Puritan interest in democratic ideas and respect for English legal institutions typified American thought. But the Puritan political revolution was only a side effect of the spiritual regeneration that lay at the heart of the movement.

> The Puritan demanded of himself—and of others—a reformation of character, the rejection of idle recreations and vain display, and sober, obedient godliness. . . . The Puritan preacher sought nothing less than a new kind of Englishman . . . [through] "a revolution of the saints."[15]

Not all Americans were Puritans, but most colonists believed in the Reformation teachings and felt a "calling" that made them "more serious, purposeful, and responsible in both [their] civic and economic roles."[16] This deep religiosity that linked the secular to the religious created a respect for law and social order which survived long after the quest for personal holiness had been abandoned.[17]

The radical theology of Puritanism was widely abandoned by the Americans of the late eighteenth century; "the values and precepts derived from it, however, remained intact,"[18] as characterized by the writings of political radicals through the Revolutionary period.

Two later developments in the spiritual and political outlook of the Revolutionary generation need to be recognized. The religious revivals of the Great Awakening, 1740–90, prepared the common people to challenge constituted authorities and defend their precious liberties. They "also intensified the general tendency of the Reformed tradition . . . to set bounds on the will of Kings and the arbitrary exercise of governmental power."[19] The intellectual developments of the Enlightenment combined with this unique religious background to produce new conceptions of freedom and equality which "were woven into the very texture of American thinking" through the discourses "of the nation's Patriot heroes and Founding Fathers."[20] Any arguments about new political institutions depended heavily on whatever support they might derive from that unique moral and religious tradition which distinguished America from every other nation on earth.

It is easy for us to recognize the hand of God in the raising up of a group of luminaries, truly wise men who labored long to inform, persuade, provoke, and lead the American people, first to independence and finally to a happy Union. But we often forget the essential role that thousands of unremembered Americans played in the invention of the new political concepts, institutions, and perceptions of an ideal society which distinguished the final document. The actual drafters of the Constitution performed a miraculous task. But it would have been impossible without the understanding support of their fellow countrymen and the rich and varied background of political experimentation and discussion on the local level over the preceding decades.

Latter-day Saints have clear scriptural evidence for expecting something extraordinary from those who have come from foreign lands to settle in America. Anciently, Lehi prophesied many things about this land and the people who should come here:

Yea, the Lord hath covenanted this land unto me, and to my children forever, and also *all those who should be led out of other countries by the hand of the Lord.*

Wherefore, I, Lehi, prophesy according to the workings of the Spirit which is in me, that there shall *none come into this land save they shall be brought by the hand of the Lord.*

Wherefore, *this land is consecrated unto him whom he shall bring.* And if it so be that they shall serve him according to the commandments which he hath given, it shall be *a land of liberty* unto them (2 Nephi 1:5–7; italics added)

The modern Americans referred to in this and other passages were a select lot whose general devotion to liberty provided the seedbed for our remarkable Constitution. The written document only reflects the most self-conscious stage of a developmental process that had been under way for generations in America. As the Americans struggled throughout the colonial and Confederation periods to shape instruments of government that would protect their individual liberties while effectively serving the public interest, they experimented endlessly in the refinement of institutions and principles which found their way, explicitly or implicitly, into that summary document. These early Americans were guided by certain principles and ideals of government which they were trying to actualize and institutionalize, as they engaged in extensive experimentation at each level of colonial government. The question is whether there was inspiration in this highly decentralized evolutionary process.

Another Model for Inspiration

It has often been observed that it is not entirely clear what is meant when one says that the Constitution is inspired. No one claims that the authors of the Constitution were prophets in the sense in which that word is used to describe the men from whom we ordinarily accept scripture. Nor did the Founding Fathers claim to be prophets. They did not claim to have seen visions, nor to have received the Constitution in any supernatural way.[21] Further, the records that we have of the federal convention make it very clear that it was not like a council meeting of Church leaders, with divinely constituted priesthood authority present to make the decisions. And, the actual phrasing that was eventually approved was the result of numerous hard-fought compromises.[22] Yet, if we take seriously the statements of the prophets on the origins of the Constitution, we must recognize that its development was divinely managed, even if in some less direct way.[23]

The Old Testament gives us an example of a society living by laws which were given directly to men by God. When the Lord appeared to Moses on the mountain, "all the people saw the thunderings, and the lightnings, and the noise of the trumpet, and the mountain smoking" (Exodus 20:18). In addition to the Ten Commandments, Moses received at the same time numerous detailed statutes to govern the daily life of the Israelites.[24]

The Book of Mormon provides the intermediate example of King Mosiah, the prophet who proposed a new constitution without claiming a detailed revelation. But we would not hesitate to call it an inspired arrangement.[25] In the case of the American Constitution, however, there was neither direct divine manifestation, nor were the principal actors prophets. Yet, like the Lamanites, they may have been blessed with the Holy Ghost and "knew it not" (3 Nephi 9:20).[26]

In our search for evidence of inspiration in the development of the Constitution, we would do well to keep in mind a modern analogy. The way in which the institutional devices and principles ultimately embodied in the Constitution developed over seventy years in American experience is very similar to the development of the present welfare program and other programs in the Church. From the very small beginning forty years ago, the Church has now developed an extensive, fully operational program to help its poor. As with our Constitution, so also the emergence of this program is marked most clearly by—

1. an experimental approach whereby successful ideas tried on the local level have eventually been incorporated into the structure of the overall program;
2. a dogged loyalty to the fundamental principles (such as that every welfare recipient shall provide some service in exchange for the commodities he receives, and that the service and commodities shall, where practicable, be provided through labor of Church members, and not by cash contribution alone);
3. a final crystallization by those authorized to establish general policies.

Members of the Church would not hesitate to say that the present Welfare Services is an inspired program. Yet it was developed first by individuals who had specific Church responsibilities to fulfill and guiding principles of love, industry, and self-respect to observe in the performance of those assignments.[27] As good and even inspired ideas came to these individuals, they were tried, found true, and adopted as part of the general Church program that is continually being organized and reorganized under the leadership of men called and sustained to that responsibility. There is inspiration both in the initiative of the individuals seeking to magnify their specific Church callings and in the adoption and improvement of new programs by general Church leaders.

Other examples of similar inspiration include the youth programs, the Church Educational System, and the prospective elders program. Each is inspired; each has undergone significant and continuing changes over the past decade or more. Most of these changes arose initially where local priesthood leaders felt impressed to adapt the general Church program to their particular circumstances in keeping with their callings.[28]

Certainly there are numerous examples of inspired programs which are simply handed down through the Church hierarchy, without prior experimentation. And certainly many programs which arise experimentally in stakes and wards are never adopted into the general Church program. Nevertheless, this remains a very important kind of inspiration which may have helped produce our "inspired Constitution." The political history of seventeenth- and eighteenth-century America shows that our Constitution emerged from the efforts of a whole people to resolve the conflict between individual liberty and political order, as well as from the creative pens of individual draftsmen.[29]

Limitation of Power as a Guiding Principle in the Evolution of Eighteenth-Century American Political Order

Eighteenth-century Americans were preoccupied with the threat of arbitrary power. Their political energies were continually devoted to the erection and protection of political and governmental devices designed to protect them from the arbitrary wills of the officers of the Crown and of their fellow Americans. While on the other hand they were extremely proud of the magnificent achievement of the mixed constitution of seventeenth- and eighteenth-century England, they saw almost everywhere means by which individuals in power could be corrupted, thus turning the government power against the people in the interest of a few.

Political radicals in England since the time of the English Civil War had voiced the dangers of power and corruption to the freedom of the individual. The second quarter of the eighteenth century saw the propaganda and political analysis of this radical opposition transplanted wholesale to the American colonies. The English radical writers—Sidney, Trenchard, Gordon, and Bolingbroke, among others—were extensively republished in the colonies and were very popularly received. Their attack centered on the corruption of the constitution and the government by the Crown and on the corruption of the people and the times in general. One leading historian has marshalled what he describes as "profuse and unmistakable" evidence that the "opposition vision of English politics, conveyed through these popular opposition writers, was determinative of the political understanding of eighteenth-century Americans."[30] The Americans universally accepted the view of the English radical that

> man was by nature lustful, that he was utterly untrustworthy in power, unable to control his passion for domination. The antinomy of power and liberty was accepted as the central fact of politics, and with it the belief that power was aggressive, liberty passive, and that the duty of free men was to protect the latter and constrain the former. Threats to free government, it was believed, lurked everywhere, but nowhere more dangerously than in the designs of ministers in office to aggrandize power by the corrupt use of influence, and by this means ultimately to destroy the balance of the constitution. Corruption, especially in the form of the manipulation and the bribery of the Commons by the gift of places, pensions, and sinecures, was as universal a cry in the colonies as it was in England, and with it the same sense of despair at the state of the rest of the world, the same belief that tyranny, already dominant over most of the earth, was continuing to spread its menace and was threatening even that greatest bastion of liberty, England itself.[31]

The primary guiding principle of the Americans was that no Englishman (especially an American heir to the rights of Englishmen) should be subjected to the arbitrary will of another man. Although they considered government to be necessary to protect individuals in the pursuit of property and happiness, they realized that it had been obviously perverted throughout history to enable those in power to impose their wills on others. As the Founding Fathers assumed that it was in the nature of all men to take advantage of political office to increase their personal wealth and power, they therefore developed institutional structures for the United States that were designed to play off the greed of one office holder against that of another. The very point of the separation of powers and system of checks and balances was to deny governmental officers the power to carry out schemes that could enhance them personally to the detriment of the people.[32] The limitation of power was indeed the theme of much of the experimentation and reasoning that led to the constitutional provisions. Whereas the mixed government of England theoretically met this function by balancing king, lords, and the commons, American society was not naturally divided this way, and new institutional devices needed to be developed.[33]

The political experimentation in America during the first century and a half of colonial experience was primarily oriented toward developing the independence of the colonial legislatures. This independence was achieved by a number of practical arrangements worked out between the legislatures and the colonial governors, and not by any formal written constitutional revisions. Many of the arrangements that the popularly elected legislatures eventually forced on the king's governors were actually illegal in terms of the charters and constitutions under which the colonial governments operated.

Greene documents nicely how these developments came about in the four southern colonies, showing that as in the other colonies, the lower houses had achieved not only equality with the crown's officers, but even superiority to them.[34] Although the formal documents had not been rewritten to accommodate new arrangements, they became solidly established in practice to resolve particular problems in ways that would be satisfactory to the colonists.

From the late 1600s to the Revolution, the colonial assemblies claimed the rights that Parliament had won in England in its struggle with the Stuarts. These included the full right of local legislation, control over both taxes and expenditures, the right to fix the qualifications of eligibility of House members, the power to apportion legislative districts, freedom of debate, immunity from arrest, and the right of the assemblies to choose their own speakers. "In Britain, these privileges had been fully vindicated by the Glorious Revolution, and in insisting upon them the colonial assemblies believed that they were assuming the normal prerogatives of all sovereign legislative bodies."[35] Of course, English officials were quick to oppose these claims, arguing that colonial legislators were more dependent on royal discretion and did not automatically enjoy the benefits gained by Parliament in the Glorious Revolution. The success of colonial legislatures in imposing their control over taxation and expenditures, however, enabled them eventually to establish all of their claims. "The victory over the purse strings, recapitulating as it did a like victory by the House of Commons over the Crown, was of tremendous importance in the growth of colonial internal autonomy."[36]

The idea of legislative independence in the colonial assemblies was never compatible with the ideals of centralized administration of the empire that were long held by London officials. By the 1760s, when the Crown decided to pursue more strictly its ideal of an efficiently organized empire, it was too late. The Americans regarded their new independence and privileges as constitutional in every way, and saw the attempts of the British government to resurrect centralized colonial administration as an attempt to deny them their constitutional rights as Englishmen[37] and enslave them.[38] Small wonder that with the success of the Revolution the thirteen states agreed on a form of national government which exalted above all things the independence of the state legislatures. This outstanding feature of the Articles of Confederation appeared to be the realization of the spoken and unspoken, recognized and unrecognized objectives of generations of Americans.

But the Union was barely born before the inadequacies of that first constitution became apparent. The jealous state legislatures had allowed the central government no power to tax and thereby finance centralized functions. Furthermore, no power was conceded to the central government by which it might exercise regulation over commerce or the economy. The statutes that the Confederation might adopt were unenforceable, as there was no recognized supremacy in its statutes over the statutes of any particular state. There was no central judiciary by which the conflicts of law might be settled nor by which residents of one state might seek redress in the courts of another. There was no central executive, and this resulted in considerable disunity. The states were virtually sovereign and could go their own way whenever they disagreed with a majority vote of Congress. There was no federal mechanism which could settle disputes arising between state and national authorities. There was no popular representation in the national congress, each state having equal representation regardless of size or population. Finally, the jealousy of the states was again emphasized in the crippling amendment procedure which required unanimous assent. The adoption of the Articles of Confederation in the first place had apparently been dependent on this absolute control by each state over any future change in that arrangement.

These defects were soon generally recognized.[39] Consequently, the short career of the Confederation was marked by continued experimentation and theoretical discussion on both the state and national levels, which in turn generated many of the political ideas and institutional devices that were eventually embodied in the Constitution. As one prominent historian observed:

> No matter how much the members might talk about democracy in theory or about ancient confederacies, when it came to action they did not go

outside of their own experience. The Constitution was devised to correct well-known defects and it contained few provisions which had not been tested by practical political experience. Before the Convention met, some of the leading men in the country had prepared lists of the defects which existed in the Articles of Confederation, and in the Constitution. Practically every one of these defects was corrected, and by means which had already been tested in the States and under the Articles of Confederation.[40]

Other constitutional historians have summarized the same point as follows:

The [colonial] era closed with the ratification of the Constitution, a document embodying the political experience of the preceding two centuries.[41]

Some Latter-day Saints seem to take the prophetic teaching that the Constitution was inspired as a reason for insisting that the original document was a final achievement, which should never be modified or revised. This seems clearly mistaken. First, the Constitution condoned slavery, a practice rejected in modern scripture.[42] But of course the Union of 1787 would not have been politically possible with a strong antislavery clause. Other defects of the original document were once outlined by Joseph Smith.[43] Second, the original document itself provides a formal amending procedure, which was promptly used to adopt the Bill of Rights. Third, serious students of the Constitution find that one of the greatest strengths of the document, which has enabled it to weather the shifting tides of American politics, ideologies, and social change is its vagueness and ambiguity in many key passages.[44] One may object to some of the fruits of this tradition of constitutional interpretation, without denying its importance to constitutional vitality. Fourth, the idea of a fixed and unchangeable Constitution seems inconsistent with the experimental origins of the document. The Americans of the nineteenth century were experimentalists in government, and the Constitution was their grand experiment. But it was not designed to end all experiments. Brigham Young explicitly recognized all this when he taught:

The signers of the Declaration of Independence and the framers of the Constitution were inspired from on high to do that work. But was that which was given to them perfect, not admitting of any addition whatever? No; for if men know anything, they must know that the Almighty has never yet found a man in mortality that was capable, at the first intimation, at the first impulse, to receive anything in a state of entire perfection. They laid the foundation, and it was for after generations to rear the superstructure upon it. It is a progressive—a gradual work.[45]

Society under the Constitution is not static; it can develop increased or decreased respect for its basic principles. The original document was flexible enough to absorb shifts in either direction. The subsequent elimination of slavery certainly represented a shift that was already taking place in the views of the American public in the direction of increased liberty. However, the example of growing economic and other regulation in the twentieth century seems to signal a dwindling commitment to rule of law, not simply because it is economic regulation, but because this regulation in the twentieth century seems to have been shaped more by political considerations of the moment.[46]

The Rule of Law

The Constitution (and its authors) assume the rule of law as essential to a free society. The point of the rule of law is to enable individuals to pursue their own ends, without fear of being frustrated by impositions of the arbitrary will of others. F. A. Hayek has explained how man can be free *and* ruled by law:

> Provided that I know beforehand that if I place myself in a particular position I shall be coerced and provided that I can avoid putting myself in such a position, I need never be coerced. At least insofar as the rules providing for coercion are not aimed at me personally but are so framed as to apply equally to all people in similar circumstances, they are no different from any of the natural obstacles that affect my plans. In that they tell me what will happen *if* I do this or that, the laws of the state have the same significance for me as the laws of nature; and I can use my knowledge of the laws of the state to achieve my own aims as I use my knowledge of the laws of nature.[47]

Legal philosophers traditionally contrast this notion of rule of law with the rule of men, which is more common in human societies. The point is that individuals are free in a system where all men are ruled by the same laws according to their common agreement; men are not free when they are subject to the whims and discretionary commands of human rulers. The authors of the American Constitution were extremely sensitive to the latter possibility and built into this document every possible safeguard—or to use Madison's phrase, every "auxiliary precaution"—against the encroachments of tyranny.

To operate fully in all dimensions of a society's legal experience, the rule of law must be attended by a number of supporting principles—all of which have been recognized to some degree in Anglo-American law. F. A. Hayek and Lon Fuller find an implicit set of rules that must be observed by a society and its government if, in fact, rule of law is to be preserved.[48] These conditions include the requirements (1) that laws be general, applying equally to all members of society, including those who enact or enforce the law; (2) that laws never apply retroactive penalties; (3) that all laws be enacted publicly, never in secret; (4) that the judges be independent of the other branches of government; (5) that administrators not be allowed discretion in applying the law to individuals; and (6) that free individual activity can only be limited by *general* rules applying equally to all. These metalegal rules are in most cases general characterizations of specific limitations placed on government, especially in Anglo-American legal history.[49]

The rule of law does not guarantee economic security, social status, or even minimal happiness to anyone. Thus it should not be confused either with the utopian scheme of the worldly philosophers or the divine outline of the City of God. Recognizing the human impossibility of the former and the present lack of the latter, the authors of our Constitution wisely selected as their guiding principle the rule of law which guarantees us nothing more than the *absence* of arbitrary coercion. Of course, the rule of law does not imply any general prohibition against affirmative government action in the protection of individuals or in pursuit of the general welfare. Rather it simply marks out certain limits to the use of any governmental coercion. Nothing is guaranteed to us except the freedom to pursue our objectives by our own individual or group efforts within certain constitutional limits. This seems to be the same point Hugh Nibley was making when he said:

> The best of human laws leaves every man free to engage in his own pursuit of happiness, without presuming for a moment to tell him where that happiness lies; that is the very thing the laws of God can guarantee. At *best*, the political prize is negative.[50]

The rule of law does nothing more than restrict governmental coercion to those special cases in which certain formal criteria are met. Students of liberty often disagree on the adequacy of the formal rule by itself. Some believe that the formal principle of rule of law needs support in constitutional declarations of certain inviolable substantive freedoms, such as freedom of religion, freedom of the press, and right to trial by jury. The authors of the Constitution had chosen to omit such declarations of substantive rights for fear that future courts might treat such a list as exhaustive.[51] As Hamilton and others persuaded their brethren in Philadelphia, the Constitution was designed to set out the limits of governmental power, not to limit the freedoms of the people.[52]

But Madison spoke for the eventual majority who preferred some explicit constitutional status for those key liberties that Englishmen had won from their king over the preceding centuries. He recognized Hamilton's argument that Americans would have no king to worry about. But he felt that insufficient attention had been given to the fact that in a democracy

> the invasion of private rights is *chiefly* to be apprehended, not from acts of Government contrary to the sense of its constituents, but from acts in which the Government is the mere instrument of the major number of the Constituents.[53]

Madison's view was widely shared, and it was only by promising to immediately append a bill of rights that the Federalists were able to obtain ratification in several states.

It is also important to note that the rule of law is a metalegal principle. That means it cannot be legislated or enacted as a safeguard for freedom, because anything that can be written into the law can be deleted from the law. Rather, to be operative in any political society, the rule of law must spring from a moral consensus of the people. It must not only be an assumption of the Constitution, but of the people governed by the Constitution.[54] It was thus crucial to the establishment of the Constitution and the rule of law in America that the population have a special character, that is, that it be selected for its love of liberty and be raised up with devotion to the rule of law.

The obvious problem is that there is no way to enforce liberty. Being free entails absence of coercion. Consequently, a legal system can only provide freedom for a population that will voluntarily espouse the principles of liberty. Without this there could be no liberty, but only force. There are numerous examples of developing countries that have admired the American Constitution, adopted its form of government, and still lapsed into dictatorships. The usual explanation is that the political culture lacked traditional commitment to "the rights of Englishmen," as it were, thus robbing the constitutional form of its vital force. A contemporary reaffirmation of this view is given to us by Russia's Aleksandr Solzhenitsyn, who sees the lack of love for liberty or traditional respect for the principles of rule of law among his people as a major reason for their failure to resist the mass imprisonment of innocent citizens that has continued over the past fifty years.[55] In an age of revolution the Americans were the only ones to exercise restrained sovereignty, stepping back to be ruled by their own legal creation. R. R. Palmer concluded that this approach was "distinctively American":

> European thinkers, in all their discussion of a political or social contract, of government by consent of sovereignty of the people, had not clearly imagined the people as actually contriving a constitution and creating the organs of government. They lacked the idea of a people as a constituent power.[56]

The rule of law guarantees a people freedom to pursue their own ends without constraint from the arbitrary will of others, a guarantee which also enables men to assume moral responsibility for their own actions. A close reading of section 101 of the Doctrine and Covenants suggests that the Constitution and the laws of America are acceptable before the Lord precisely because they are established "*according to* just and holy principles" (D&C 101:77; italics added). And what is the effect of these principles? The same as the effect of the rule of law!

> That every man may act in doctrine and principle pertaining to futurity, according to the moral agency which I have given unto him, that every man may be accountable for his own sins in the day of judgment. (D&C 101:78)

This verse seems to echo the common sentiment that men are morally responsible for their acts only when they are free from the arbitrary compulsion of others. Thus a man is only responsible for his own sins (or acts of righteousness) when he is free to "act in doctrine and principle pertaining to futurity," that is, when the future consequence of his acts can be reasonably predicted in the light of previous experience and known rules, without being governed arbitrarily by the will of others. But this means that the rule of law is at the least functionally equivalent to the "just and holy principles" referred to in the scripture. The same principle which makes men responsible for their own sins also makes them free to pursue wealth or happiness in any other form. An inspired constitution embracing that principle could be established by the hands of "wise men" whose motives might vary dramatically from the motives of righteous prophets. Yet each gets the results he desires.[57]

Just as it was necessary to devise a substantially new institutional device to preserve the ancient rights and liberties of Englishmen in the new and unique egalitarian society of eighteenth-century America, so we might find that other forms of government could well be established "according to just and holy principles" in nations with different political cultures or social compositions. King Benjamin proved that all the requirements of the rule of law could be met in a righteous monarchy. His successors went on to establish a government composed only of elected judges which proved able to preserve the same principles for several generations. Another Book of Mormon prophet saw exactly the same principles as essential, combining in one statement the ends of moral responsibility and personal freedom as achievements of good law. As Mosiah writes:

> I command you to do these things, and that ye have no king; that if these people commit sins and iniquities they shall be answered upon their own heads.
> For behold I say unto you, the sins of many people have been caused by the iniquities of their kings; therefore their iniquities are answered upon the heads of their kings.
> And now I desire that this inequality should be no more in this land, especially among this my people; but I desire that this land be a land of liberty, and every man enjoy his rights and privileges alike. (Mosiah 29:30–32)

Liberty Dependent on Morality

The inspired principles in the Constitution are the principles of the rule of law which, if preserved, guarantee liberty to every man. These principles are assumed in the Constitution because they had come to be assumed by Americans generally, as they struggled through several generations to find institutional safeguards for the liberty that they prized so highly. Many theoreticians of law and politics have rejected such a tenuous and fragile basis for a nation's freedom. They dream of constitutional arrangements based on clear libertarian principles which would maximize individual liberty whether or not the people understood or supported the basic principles. Their objection does raise the important secondary problem of preserving the liberty we have obtained.

The early Americans themselves recognized the necessity of "public virtue" for the continuing security of their liberty. As a recent prize-winning history summarizes:

> In a monarchy, each man's desire to do what is right in his own eyes could be restrained by fear or force. In a Republic, however, each man must somehow be persuaded to submerge his personal wants into the

greater good of the whole. This willingness of the individual to sacrifice his private interest for the good of the community—such patriotism or love of country—the eighteenth century termed public virtue. A republic was such a delicate polity precisely because it demanded such an extraordinary moral character in the people. Every state in which the people participated needed a degree of virtue; but a republic which rested solely on the people absolutely required it, although a particular structural arrangement of the government in a republic might temper the necessity for public virtue, ultimately no model of government whatever can equal the importance of this principle, nor afford proper safety and security without it.

Without some portion of this generous principle, anarchy and confusion would immediately ensue. The jarring interest of individuals, regarding themselves only, and indifferent to the welfare of others would still further heighten the distressing scene, and with the assistance of the selfish passions, it would end in the ruin and subversion of the state. The eighteenth century mind was thoroughly convinced that a popularly based government "cannot be supported without virtue." Only with a public-spirited, self-sacrificing people would the authority of a popularly elected rule be obeyed, but "more by the virtue of the people than by the terror of his power." Because virtue is truly the lifeblood of the republic, the thoughts and hopes surrounding the concept of public spirit gave the Revolution its socially radical character—an expected alteration in the very behavior of the people "laying the foundation in a constitution, not without or over, but within the subjects."[58]

This teaching is appropriately extended by Mosiah's warning:

> Now it is not common that the voice of the people desireth anything contrary to that which is right; but it is common for the lesser part of the people to desire that which is not right; therefore this shall ye observe and make it your law—to do your business by the voice of the people.
>
> And if the time comes that the voice of the people doth choose iniquity, then is the time that the judgments of God will come upon you; yea, then is the time he will visit you with great destruction even as he has hitherto visited this land. (Mosiah 29:26–27)

The Constitution and the Saints

No matter what happens with the rest of the gentiles, if the Latter-day Saints are righteous and love liberty, the Constitution will be preserved among them, and as liberty declines elsewhere, it will shine forth more and more brightly among them as a beacon, drawing the honest in heart and lovers of liberty from all the earth to Zion. As John Taylor prophesied in 1879:

We have got to establish a government upon the principle of righteousness, justice, truth and equality and not according to the many false notions that exist among men. And then the day is not far distant when this nation will be shaken from centre to circumference. And now, you may write it down, any of you, and I will prophesy it in the name of God. And then will be fulfilled the prediction to be found in one of the revelations given through the Prophet Joseph Smith. Those who will not take up their sword to fight against their neighbor must needs flee to Zion for safety. And they will come, saying, we do not know anything of the principles of your religion, but we perceive that you are an honest community; you administer justice and righteousness, and we want to live with you and receive the protection of your laws, but as for your religion we will talk about that some other time. Will we protect such people? Yes, all honorable men. When the people shall have torn to shreds the Constitution of the United States the Elders of Israel will be found holding it up to the nations of the earth, and proclaiming liberty and equal rights to all men, and extending the hand of fellowship to the oppressed of all nations. This is part of the programme, and as long as we do what is right and fear God, he will help us and stand by us under all circumstances.[59]

The eighteenth-century radicals that perpetrated the American Revolution were often highly respected men of substance and were widely regarded as moral leaders in their communities. They were usually leaders in the popular party serving as elected representatives in assemblies and other posts of public trust. Their radical creed was characterized by a deep and passionate opposition to arbitrary and uncontrolled government—by a love of liberty, as it has usually been called. We have been warned by contemporary prophets not to associate ourselves with the rhetoric or political tactics of modern radicals of the left or the right, who also wave their flags of liberty. This might seem inconsistent unless we recognize that being a radical does not entail adherence to any particular political doctrine. Rather, it refers to the depth and degree of commitment. The radicals of the left today seek freedom from social and material deprivation through the application of government power. On the right, according to your preferences in political taxonomy, we have either those libertarians who would go far beyond the classically liberal views of the Founding Fathers in restricting the role of government, or those reactionaries who would be willing to invoke arbitrarily the power of government to reshape moral society in their own image. Modern prophets seem to reject both the reactionary and radical left views. And in clearly recognizing a positive role for limited government, they refuse to join the libertarians. Like those wise men who forged our Constitution they speak out for integrity in public affairs, protection of the rights of individuals from arbitrary government interference, and for loyalty to that constitutional system which has been so successful in securing to us our freedoms in the past. As we seek to teach our children to love and appreciate their liberty, we would in the contemporary context emphasize the virtues of our constitutional system, the need to protect and repair it as necessary, and the importance of holding public officials to strict standards of integrity, allowing no man to stand above the law. Perhaps the most important things we can do to preserve our constitution and our liberty are first to learn to understand and love liberty ourselves and then to teach our children and our fellow citizens these same things.[60] Indeed we might do well to follow the exhortation of young Abraham Lincoln, who urged his hearers to make the love of liberty and the respect for law "the political religion of the nation."[61]

The Book of Mormon teaches that our continued liberty in this land depends on our obedience to Christ's commandments. Therefore, we can make our most important contribution to the preservation of national liberty by calling on our nation to repent and come unto Christ. The Constitution of the United States is seriously threatened by the widespread lack of understanding of and loyalty to its fundamental principles. If modern Americans, who have received their constitutional heritage as a free gift, can be helped to understand and support it with the same fervor as have many generations of immigrants, we will have no need to fear for the future.

---

1. Clinton Rossiter, "The American Mission," *American Scholar* 20 (1950–51): 19.

2. Conrad Cherry, *God's New Israel: Religious Interpretations of American Destiny* (Englewood Cliffs, N. J.: Prentice-Hall, 1971), p. 23. From this study of the holy scriptures, Puritans "recognized that governments, and laws were instituted to restrain man's sin and hence were truly of God." Sydney E. Ahlstrom, *A Religious History of the American People* (New Haven, Conn.: Yale University Press, 1972), p. 129.

3. See, for example, George Bancroft, *History of the United States from the Discovery of the American Continent* (Boston: Charles Bowen, 1837).

4. See generally Cherry, *God's New Israel,* and specifically his preface, pp. vii–viii. An interesting exception to this prevailing view is represented by the anthology edited by Frederick Gentles and Marvin Steinfield innocently titled *Dream On, America* (San Francisco: Canfield Press, 1971). Incidentally, Gentles and Steinfield reprint a feature article from the *Los Angeles Times* by John Dart on Brigham Young University to give an example of a university and a people that have preserved the central elements of the American dream ("A Campus of Peace and Patriotism," pp. 67–73).

5. Elder L. Tom Perry and his assistant Richard W. Eyre recently attended a planning meeting of the American Revolution Bicentennial Association along with representatives of 200 other American religious organizations. They encountered "uniform opposition" to their efforts to encourage the association to "place some emphasis on the religious aspects of this nation's birth," including the feeling that both the Declaration of Independence and the Constitution were inspired documents. I am indebted to Richard W. Eyre for this information provided by letter, 18 July 1975.

6. Other typical affirmations published by Church leaders include: Brigham Young in *Journal of Discourses* 26 vols. (London: Latter-day Saints Book Depot, 1855–86), 7:13–15 (hereafter cited as *JD*); J. Reuben Clark, Jr., *Conference Report*, April 1935, p. 93; Heber J. Grant, *Improvement Era* 43 (1940):127; and George Albert Smith, *Conference Report*, April 1940, p. 85.

7. From a generally distributed letter clarifying the Church position regarding Negroes, signed for the First Presidency by Hugh B. Brown and N. Eldon Tanner and dated 15 December 1969; published in *Improvement Era* 73 (February 1970): 70. See also note 57 below.

8. See, for example, Charles Beard, *Economic Interpretations of the Constitution of the United States* (New York: Macmillan, 1962).

9. The most important work on Beard's thesis is Robert E. Brown, *Charles Beard and the Constitution* (Princeton, N.J.: Princeton University Press, 1956).

10. Henry Steele Commager, "Leadership in Eighteenth-Century America and Today," *Freedom and Order* (New York: G. Braziller, 1966), pp. 149–50.

11. Bernard Bailyn, *Ideological Origins of the American Revolution* (Cambridge, Mass.: Harvard University Press, 1967), pp. 1–8.

12. This quotation from La Rochefocault-Liancourt, *Travels*, 2:215, is taken from Jackson Turner Main's study *The Social Structure of Revolutionary America* (Princeton, N. J.: Princeton University Press, 1965), p. 254. Main reports several studies of inventories and probate records that further support the view that Americans in the North *and* the South were surprisingly well read (pp. 253–55).

13. See, generally, Kenneth Lockenridge, *Literacy in Colonial New England* (New York: Norton, 1974).

14. Ahlstrom, *Religious History of the American People*, p. 124. This same historian claims that the legacy of Puritanism in America was "no less significant than the impact of Luther upon the German nation " (Ibid., p. 98).

15. Ibid., p. 129.

16. Ibid., p. 348.

17. "Puritanism . . . virtually sacrificed itself on the altar of civic responsibility. It helped to create a nation of individuals who were also fervent 'moral athletes,' with a strong sense of transcendent values which must receive ordered and corporate expression in the commonwealth" (Ibid., p. 348).

18. Edmund S. Morgan, "The Puritan Ethic and the American Revolution," *William and Mary Quarterly*, 3d. ser. 24 (January 1967):6.

19. Ahlstrom, *Religious History of the American People*, p. 350.

20. Ibid., p. 362.

21. An exception of possible significance occurs in *Federalist* 37, by James Madison. Near the end of that essay, Madison marvels at the purity of the document brought forth under such adverse circumstances and concludes that "it is impossible for the man of pious reflection not to perceive in it a finger of that Almighty hand which has been so frequently and signally extended to our relief in the critical stages of the revolution" (*The Federalist Papers*, ed. Clinton Rossiter [New York: New American Library, 1961], pp. 230–31.

22. Charles Biddle, who was acquainted with most of the members of this convention, claimed that some of the best-informed members of the federal convention had told him "they did not believe a single member was *perfectly* satisfied with the Constitution, but they believed it was the best they could ever agree upon, and that it was infinitely better to have such a one than break up without fixing on some form of government, which I believe at one time it was expected they would have done" (as quoted from Biddle's *Autobiography* in Max Farrand, *The Fathers of the Constitution* [New Haven, Conn.: Yale University Press, 1921], p. 141).

23. President J. Reuben Clark, Jr., observed that the Founding Fathers were "in God's hand; he guided them in their epoch making deliberations in Independence Hall" (*Conference Report*, April 1957, p. 48). But he saw in their work "the culmination of a long historical process which had its beginnings deep in the efforts of the English people to free themselves from the tyranny of absolute monarchy" (Martin B. Hickman, "J. Reuben Clark, Jr.: The Constitution and the Great Fundamentals," *J. Reuben Clark, Jr.: Diplomat and Statesman*, ed. Ray C. Hillam [Provo, Utah: Brigham Young University Press, 1973], p. 32).

24. See especially Exodus 21 and 22 for good examples of this.

25. See generally Mosiah 29.

26. It would be a serious mistake to underrate this inspiration in light of the Savior's promise to pour out the Holy Ghost on the gentiles, making them "mighty above all" unto the scattering of the Israelites (3 Nephi 20:27).

27. Additional insight into this well-known example is provided by a letter written to President Spencer W. Kimball, 12 June 1971, by Paul C. Child, who was called to be a counselor to President Harold B. Lee when the Pioneer Stake was reorganized in 1930. At that time President Child was given the responsibility for developing a welfare program for the Pioneer Stake.

In this letter, President Child explains how the program developed as opportunities arose providing means by which the needs of the unemployed members of the Pioneer Stake might be met. He gives numerous examples of the explicit dependence of the stake presidency on the scriptures, the words of the prophet, and on their own inspiration. He also records how the Pioneer Stake program proved to be the answer to the needs of the Church as the First Presidency undertook to develop such a program on a Churchwide basis (Paul C. Child, "Physical Beginning of the Church Welfare Program," *BYU Studies* [Spring 1974], pp. 383–86).

28. This phenomenon has been labeled "creative stewardship" by W. Keith Warner and Edward L. Kimball ("Creative Stewardship," *The Carpenter* 1 [Spring 1971]: 17–26). In this insightful article, Warner and Kimball analyze not only the process, but the doctrinal support for it as well. They also have several examples that illustrate how local leadership can create inspired programs, some of which ultimately prove suitable for general Church use. Their intent is to encourage Church members "not only to be willing workers, but also to be creative stewards" (p. 26).

Good scriptural support for this notion of individual revelation comes from D&C 58:24–29. Edward Partridge and his associates had been commanded to go to Zion and after some delay had inquired of Joseph Smith as to the means by which they should travel. The

Lord's reply instructs Edward Partridge to seek the direction of the Lord personally. "Let them bring their families to this land, *as they shall counsel between themselves and me*" (v. 25). "For *the power is in them* wherein they are agents unto themselves" (v. 28). This seems to suggest that the power in them, or the Holy Ghost, will aid them as they counsel between themselves and their Father in heaven to find his will in this matter. On this occasion, the Lord took time to expand upon the principle underlying his reply, explaining that "it is not meet that I should command in all things [presumably through the Prophet]; for he that is compelled in all things, the same is a slothful and not a wise servant. . . . Men should be anxiously engaged in a good cause, and do many things of their own free will, and bring to pass much righteousness" (vs. 26–27). In this instance we have a clear example of a Church member being told not to seek complete direction from the head of the Church in carrying out his assignment, but to seek that direction from the Lord himself.

This teaching is supported by the instructions given to Oliver Cowdery in section 9 of the Doctrine and Covenants. Oliver had failed to "continue as [he had] commenced" to translate the record because he had "supposed that I would give it unto you, when you took no thought save it was to ask me" (vs. 5, 7). The Lord goes on to explain that the individual must exert his own efforts in resolving the problem before he calls upon the Lord for inspiration. "But behold, I say unto you, that you must study it out in your mind; then you must ask me if it be right, and if it be right I will cause that your bosom shall burn within you; therefore, you shall feel that it is right" (v. 8). Or as Oliver was promised earlier, "I will tell you in your mind and in your heart, by the Holy Ghost, which shall come upon you" (D&C 8:2).

29. This evolutionary view of the formulation of the Constitution is not original. As Martin Hickman has observed, "There is nothing in President [J. Reuben] Clark's writings on the Constitution which suggests that he thought the whole of the drama of the Constitution was played in Philadelphia in 1787. Rather he saw the Constitution as emerging from a long historical process. President Clark was fully aware that the political principles which are enshrined in the Constitution had their origins in the development of Anglo-Saxon legal and political experience. . . . [The framers] brought to their task, as he clearly saw, a mastery of the political ideas which had gradually emerged from the long struggle of Englishmen for self-government" (Hickman, "J. Reuben Clark," pp. 27–28).

William C. Kimball has claimed that the most important factors in the shaping of our Constitution were "the historical traditions of the English rule of law, the century and a half of unsupervised self-government, the lack of entrenched vested interest in the New World, and the literally boundless expanse of territory in which the New America could expand. In addition, one must take into consideration that the society itself was and is democratic—that is, we are all, or most of us, brought up to respect the rules of government, to support the regime, and to constantly tinker with the mechanisms of government, to adapt them to our changing needs" ("The Constitution as a Delphic Oracle." Address delivered to the Cambridge Massachusetts Institute of Religion, 10 October 1969, p. 3).

Sydney George Fisher develops in detail the view that the component elements of the Constitution were the results of a long evolutionary history in English and American politics. This view was current even at the time the Constitution was written and was clearly derived from English legal history in which all Englishmen could see the clear evolution of individual liberty through the development of more and more effective restraints on government (Sydney George Fisher, *The Evolution of the Constitution of the United States* [Philadelphia: Lippincott, 1897]).

30. Bernard Bailyn, *The Origins of American Politics* (New York: Random House, 1967), p. 56.

31. Ibid., pp. 56–57. Richard L. Bushman has corrected Bailyn's generalization somewhat by showing that colonial concern over corruption did not extend to legislatures until after 1750. Whereas the colonists had long complained of the inherent corruptibility of their appointed governors and other Crown officers, foreigners of little or no means and no vested interest in the colonies, it was only after 1750 and "under the tutelage of English radicals" that "a growing number of colonial politicians came to see that they were not part of a struggle extending

beyond their own mercenary governors." Their notion of corruption "grew from simple greed to include corruption of the legislature through patronage and electoral influence." Thus Bushman believes the Revolution was fought not only "to escape the dominion of an oppressive ministry and a corrupted Parliament but [also] to create a government of men they could trust, men whose interests mingled with their own and whose lust was checked by all the limitations on power enlightenment thinkers had devised" (Richard L. Bushman, "Corruption and Power in Provincial America," *The Development of a Revolutionary Mentality* [Washington, D. C.: Library of Congress, 1972], p. 82).

32. Cf. Bushman, p. 73, and Gerald Stourzh, *Alexander Hamilton and the Idea of Republican Government* (Stanford, Calif.: Stanford University Press, 1970), pp. 63–75.

33. Bailyn, *Origins of American Politics*, pp. 59ff.

34. Jack P. Greene, *The Quest for Power* (Chapel Hill: University of North Carolina Press, 1963). As Greene and other historians have carefully demonstrated, colonial legislatures were fantastically successful in gaining controls over finances, the payment of fees and salaries, their own legislative procedures concerning membership and internal proceedings, and control over the affairs of the executive, including the collection of revenue, public works, printers, military affairs, Indian affairs, courts and judges, and church offices. For a detailed study of similar developments in Massachusetts, see Bushman, "Corruption and Power," p. 82, who concluded: "It was that perception of power, those animosities and fears pulsing below the surface of the constitutional disputes, that compelled the assemblies to defend and enlarge their privileges."

35. Alfred H. Kelly and Winfred A. Harbison, *The American Constitution: Its Origin and Development*, 3rd ed. (New York: W. W. Norton & Co., 1963), p. 30. See also Michael G. Hall, Lawrence H. Leder, and Michael G. Kammen, eds., *The Glorious Revolution in America* (Chapel Hill: University of North Carolina Press, 1964), p. 214.

36. Kelly and Harbison, *The American Constitution*, p. 31.

37. Modern Americans may need to be reminded that the constitutional rights of eighteenth-century Englishmen were simply those liberties and privileges that had been won from the king through military or political struggle and established by general observance over the years.

38. The attitude of Americans toward these Crown policies was not fully appreciated before the Harvard historian Bernard Bailyn carefully examined the full range of political literature published in that pre-Revolutionary period. After that study, Bailyn concluded that: "We shall not understand why there was a revolution until we suspend disbelief and listen with care to what the Revolutionaries themselves said was the reason there was a revolution.

". . . We shall have much disbelief to overcome. For what the leaders of the Revolutionary movement themselves said lay behind the convulsion of the time—what they themselves said was the cause of it all—was nothing less than a deliberate 'design'—a conspiracy—of ministers of state and their underlings to overthrow the British constitution, both in England and in America, and to blot out, or at least severely reduce, English liberties" (Bailyn, *Origins of American Politics*, p. 11).

39. Hamilton appealed for support of the new Constitution by using a systematic review of the defects of the Articles of Confederation in *Federalist Papers* 21 and 22 (Rossiter, *The Federalist Papers*, pp. 138–52).

40. Farrand, *Fathers of the Constitution*, pp. 141–42.

41. Kelly and Harbison, *The American Constitution*, p. 5.

42. "It is not right that any man should be in bondage one to another" (D&C 101:79).

43. Joseph Smith, *History of The Church of Jesus Christ of Latter-day Saints*, ed. B. H. Roberts, 7 vols. (Salt Lake City: The Church of Jesus Christ of Latter-day Saints, 1932–51), 6:7.

44. For example, Rex E. Lee, first dean of the J. Reuben Clark School of Law, sees this feature of the Constitution as additional evidence of its inspiration, and as the explanation for the ability of the Constitution to function successfully over a 183-year period of "explosive growth" (Rex E. Lee, "The United States Constitution: Divinity and Controversy," Commissioner's Lecture Series [Provo, Utah: Brigham Young University Press, 1972]). Very likely much of this vagueness was deliberate. Anyone who has served on writing committees knows that vagueness is the child of compromise. See, for example, the explanation given by Gouverneur Morris for his use of vague terms in Article IV, Section 3, as quoted in Max M. Minty, *Gouverneur Morris and the Revolution* (Norman, Oklahoma: University of Oklahoma Press, 1970), p. 191.

45. *JD*, 7:13–15. As J. Reuben Clark, Jr., once stated, "It is not my belief nor is it the doctrine of my Church that the Constitution is a fully grown document. On the contrary, we believe it must grow and develop to meet the changing needs of an advancing world" (J. Reuben Clark, Jr., "Constitutional Government: Our Birthright Threatened," *Vital Speeches of the Day*, 1 January 1939, p. 177).

46. F. A. Hayek, *The Constitution of Liberty* (Chicago: University of Chicago Press, 1960), part III.

47. Ibid., p. 142.

48. See ibid., pp. 208–19, and Lon Fuller, *The Morality of Law*, rev. ed. (New Haven, Conn.: Yale University Press, 1969), pp. 33–94.

49. For an exciting yet concise historical analysis of the development of rule of law, see Francis D. Wormuth, *The Origins of Modern Constitutionalism* (New York: Harper and Row, 1949). Wormuth has influenced several other authors mentioned in this essay. His account should, however, be compared with the more traditional one by Charles Howard McIllwain, *Constitutionalism Ancient and Modern*, rev. ed. (Ithaca, N. Y.: Cornell University Press, 1947).

50. Hugh Nibley, "Beyond Politics," *BYU Studies* 15 (Autumn 1974):11. Nibley's reference to the *Teachings of the Prophet Joseph Smith* is worth repeating here: "The laws of men may guarantee to a people protection in the honorable pursuits of this life . . . and when this is said, all is said" (Joseph Fielding Smith, comp., *Teachings of the Prophet Joseph Smith* [Salt Lake City: Deseret Book, 1938], p. 50).

51. The Ninth Amendment clearly stipulates that "the enumeration of certain rights in this Constitution shall not be construed to deny or disparage others retained by the people." Some observers believe that the fears of Hamilton and Wilson have been realized as this provision has been frequently forgotten (Hayek, *Constitution of Liberty*, p. 186). The historical failure to use the Ninth Amendment has been documented and lamented by L. W. Dunbar, "James Madison and the Ninth Amendment," 42 *Virginia Law Review* 627. The utility of the Ninth Amendment has since been recognized by Justice Goldberg, who tried to develop it to support the right of privacy which is not enumerated in the Bill of Rights. See his 1964 concurring opinion in *Griswold* v. *Connecticut*, where he observed: "The Ninth Amendment to the Contitution may be regarded by some as a recent discovery and may be forgotten by others, but since 1791, it has been a basic part of the Constitution" (381 *United States Reports* 479, 491).

52. See his argument in *Federalist* 84 (Rossiter, *The Federalist Papers*), especially pp. 513–14. Also see James Wilson's argument to the Pennsylvanians in *The Debates in the Several State*

Conventions, on the Adoption of the Federal Constitution, ed. Jonathan Elliot (Philadelphia and Washington: J. B. Lippincott, 1863), 2:436, where he described the proposal for a bill of rights as "highly imprudent."

53. From a letter to Jefferson dated 17 October 1788, published by S. K. Padover, ed., *The Complete Madison* (New York: Harper, 1953), p. 254. I am indebted to Hayek's book for the references in these two footnotes.

54. Cf. Hayek, *Constitution of Liberty*, pp. 180–82.

55. Aleksandr I. Solzhenitsyn, *The Gulag Archipelago* (New York: Harper & Row, 1974). Or as he says of prisoners who are broken, "We lost the *measure of freedom*" (p. 143). Other passages emphasizing the habitual disregard of the rule of law in Soviet Russia include, pp. 15, 147–49, 151–53, 161–62, 177–78, 281–91, 298, 308–9, 329, 333, 352, 359, 367, 399, 407–8, 431, 505, 537, and 563.

56. R. R. Palmer, *The Age of Democratic Revolution*, 2 vols. (Princeton, N. J.: Princeton University Press, 1959), 1:214–15. Palmer believes that although "the American and the French revolutions 'proceeded from the same principles' . . . the difference is that these principles were much more deeply rooted in America. [The] ideas of constitutionalism, individual liberty, or legal equality—were more fully incorporated and less disputed in America than in Europe" (p. 189).

57. This analysis seems generally consistent with Hugh Nibley's essay on the "ancient law of liberty" in which he concluded that "it is more than Fourth of July rhetoric when the Latter-day Saints declare that the Constitution is an inspired document. It actually is the restoration to the earth of that ancient law of liberty which has been preached by the prophets in every age allowing every man to act in doctrine and principle according to the moral agency which God has given him, to be accountable for his own sins in the day of judgment. Such acts may never be prescribed or judged by any human agency, the Constitution maintains, and we firmly believe that to be the will of God: it was known to the early Christians as the ancient law of liberty" (Hugh Nibley, *The World and the Prophets* [Salt Lake City: Deseret Book, 1962], p. 173).

58. Gordon S. Wood, *The Creation of the American Republic, 1776–1787* (New York: W. W. Norton and Co., 1969), p. 68. See also Bushman, "Corruption and Power," p. 63, and Stourzh, *Alexander Hamilton*.

59. *JD* 21:8. Brigham Young had acknowledged much earlier that "we have the best system of government in existence, but queried if the people of this nation were righteous enough to sustain its institutions." He answered his own rhetorical question: "I say they are not, but will trample them under their feet" (*JD*, 12:119; cited in Nibley, "Beyond Politics," p. 14).

60. As Harold B. Lee has put it, "We would hope that we might be instrumental in developing statesmen—men not only with unsurpassed excellence of training in the law, but also with an unwavering faith that the Constitution of the United States was divinely inspired and written by men whom God raised up for this very purpose." And: "May I voice a plea for all Americans to love this country with a fervor that will inspire each to so live as to merit the favor of the Almighty during this time of grave uncertainties, as well as in times to come. I would that all men could believe in the destiny of America as did the early pioneers: that it is the land of Zion; that the founders of this nation were men of inspired vision; that the Constitution as written by the inspiration of heaven must be preserved at all costs.

"I will make a further plea that the citizens of this favored land live righteously that they might enjoy the fruits of their righteousness in this land of promise" (Harold B. Lee, *Ye Are the Light of the World* [Salt Lake City: Deseret Book, 1974], pp. 118, 181–82).

61. A speech at the Young Men's Lyceum, Springfield, Illinois, 27 January 1838, entitled "The Perpetuation of Our Political Institutions," *The Collected Works of Abraham Lincoln*, ed. Roy P. Basler, 8 vols. (New Brunswick, N. J.: Rutgers University Press, 1953), 1:112.

Virtue and the Constitution

Richard L. Bushman, professor of history, claims that the functioning of freedom in a constitutional democracy cannot exist without people who are virtuous. He defines virtue as the avoidance of self-indulgence and the sacrifice of personal interest for the good of the whole. Selfishness, he says, is the opposite of virtue. Bushman asserts that our constitutional system is a good mechanism for sifting out selfishness and checking human lust for power; but he warns that it is not a fail-safe system, for we need men of virtue if the system is to run well. This is also Professor Reynolds's thesis in his essay, "The Doctrine of an Inspired Constitution." Bushman's lecture concludes by asking: "How virtuous is America today?" He enjoins Mormons to be actively engaged in the political system with people of good faith and high moral standards everywhere. He further encourages the teaching of faith and virtue, calling this enterprise "the highest kind of political activity."

Professor Bushman received his undergraduate and graduate education at Harvard University, where he received his Ph.D. in history. He has been on the faculty at Brigham Young University and Boston University. He is currently chairman of the Department of History at the University of Delaware.

In the thirteenth Article of Faith, the Lord said (through the Prophet Joseph Smith) that some worldly things are lovely, praiseworthy, and of good report. The Constitution is one of these. Even though it was not given through the priesthood or by prophets, it is based upon just and holy principles and can therefore be rightfully called a part of the Mormon faith.

The Lord had to emphasize this specific point explicitly because the inherent virtue of the Constitution was not clear to the Saints in the early years of the Church. The Lord had rapidly established a new social, political, and economic order. He had revealed his law in 1831 (D&C 42) and identified Zion soon after. In short, a new kind of society was organized. In one of the revelations given in this period, the Lord told the Saints: "I say unto you that in time ye shall have no king nor ruler, for I will be your king and watch over you. . . . And you shall be a free people, and ye shall have no laws but my laws when I come" (D&C 38:21–22).

With that prospect opened to them, the Saints wondered for a moment what laws applied to them now that they were the Lord's people and not merely citizens of the United States. Thus, two years later, it was necessary for the Lord to tell the people that the "law of the land which is constitutional, supporting that principle of freedom in maintaining rights and privileges, belongs to all mankind, and is justifiable before me. Therefore, I, the Lord, justify you, and your brethren of my church, in befriending that law which is the constitutional law of the land" (D&C 98:5–6). This endorsement means that, although Mormons are primarily followers of God, they should submit to the Constitution and to other laws.

Having this statement from the Lord has been of great value because it permits Saints to take the strongest possible stand on the Constitution whenever it is endangered. It does not help much, though, in specific instances of interpretation. The Lord's comments do not illuminate the everyday affairs of politics and the courts, but they do add immense strength to the framework of government. The Lord has said that the basic constitutional principles of this country are sound. This understanding has a salutory influence on Mormons as they involve themselves in politics. It means that they can tolerate the debate, the compromises, the give and take, and all the nitty-gritty of political activity as part of their growing, necessary human experience. They can enter into this tug-of-war because they have confidence in the general rules of the game.

Men and women expend enormous amounts of physical and mental energy in an effort to win in athletic competitions. But they do it all within a very carefully framed structure. How different it would be if they were skeptical about the rules, in doubt about their justice! The verses on the Constitution in the Doctrine and Covenants endorse the framework of government and legitimize the rules of the game. In that confidence, Mormons can give their best energies to political competition, can even enjoy the melee, because they know the framework is sound.

In recent years the Latter-day Saint view of the Constitution and of American history has received support from an unexpected quarter: secular scholarship. One of the great discoveries of historians in the past decade has been the crucial importance of virtue in the minds of American revolutionaries and of those who framed the Constitution.[1] Many of the early leaders of this country were persuaded that free government could not survive unless the people were virtuous. By virtue they meant essentially two things: first, the avoidance of luxury and self-indulgence, and secondly, the sacrifice of personal interest for the good of the whole. They used patriotism as a synonym for virtue, but their definition of patriotism was different from the current definition. It did not mean loyalty to one's country in contrast to other countries of the world, but loyalty to the *country* as contrasted to the *self*. The patriot was one who served the public good rather than the private good. Kennedy's electric statement, "Ask not what your country can do for you, but what you can do for your country," was fully in the spirit of the eighteenth-century definition of patriotism or virtue. The word is currently used to cover both of these notions, and selfishness is the opposite of virtue.

The trouble with selfishness, as the framers saw it, was that a selfish person was unprepared to defend liberty when the inevitable assaults were made upon it. The commitment to pleasure so weakened the character of a self-indulgent person that when resistance to tyranny was required, he would sacrifice his liberty rather than exert himself. He would be soft rather than hard and strong, and enervated and dull rather than alert and vigilant. Or in a variant of the same theme, the greedy and avaricious person devoted solely to profit and gain would sell his liberties. The tyrant could easily buy the aid and support of the greedy person in trampling on the rights of the people.

The eighteenth century believed that these character deficiencies brought on the decline and fall of nations. Gibbon's volumes on the Roman Empire, which appeared in the middle of the century, reinforced this mode of thinking. One of the revolutionary leaders' concerns was that the new nation would follow the course of Athens and Rome through freedom and vigor into property and riches, to luxury and self-indulgence, and finally weakness, slavishness, and tyranny. Particularly in those decades immediately after independence, the political thinkers were constantly watching, observing, wondering about the character of the people. Was the nation worthy of freedom?

Through the Revolution and with deepening gloom in the following years, many of the founders lost confidence in the virtue of the American people. In January of 1776, prior to independence, John Adams wrote to Mercy Warren (one of his favorite correspondents on political matters) that nowhere did he see an American worthy of freedom. Everywhere the "Rage for Profit and Commerce," everywhere servility, flattery, and cringing before authority, rather than the noble qualities of the true patriot and citizen of a Republic.[2] Washington, who had so many opportunities to see the American people in action, was depressed after taking command of the Continental Army in Boston in July of 1775. What did he see? Soldiers who deserted before their terms of enlistment were complete, carrying off the precious guns issued to them. Provisioners who charged the highest possible prices to feed a starving army when the government was desperately short of funds. There was nothing during the war or in the 1780s to reassure Washington or Madison or Adams about American virtue. The demand for paper money, the refusal to meet the just demands of their creditors, Shays' Rebellion, and a host of other public events and private experiences convinced the leaders that the American people did not possess the hoped-for virtue.

In the summer of 1786, just one year before the Constitutional Convention, John Jay wrote to Washington: "There doubtless is much reason to think and to say that we are woefully and, in many instances, wickedly misled. Private rage for property suppresses public considerations, and personal rather than national interests have become the great objects of attention."

Washington replied a month later: "We have errors to correct. We have probably had too good an opinion of human nature in forming our Confederation. Experience has taught us, that men will not adopt and carry into execution measures the best calculated for their own good, without the intervention of a coercive power. I do not conceive we can exist long as a nation without having lodged somewhere a power, which will pervade the whole Union in as energetic a manner as the authority of the State governments extends over the several States."[3]

The Constitution, then, was an effort to compensate for lack of virtue in the American people. It would create a government which in the language of the eighteenth century would "draw to a point" the virtue of the people. Laws that punished vice and rewarded virtue, that protected the rights of the minority, might prevent freedom from deteriorating.

Many argued that the Constitution gave too much power to the central government, and that the effort to compensate for popular deficiencies put the nation in danger of tyranny. Little by little the nation was persuaded that these fears were unjustified until every state finally ratified. Among the many arguments favoring the Constitution, one received great attention: James Madison's famous argument in *Federalist* 10. The gist of it was that the problem of selfishness could be handled by permitting the various expressions of selfishness to cancel each other out. A large republic would bring into the halls of Congress so many conflicting interests that the difficulty of obtaining a majority would prevent special interest groups from having their way. All that the delegates could agree upon would be the small number of things which were truly for the good of all. Thus government would be limited. There would be many interests that simply could not be heeded: government would thus be restricted to the general good. That kind of Constitution, with those kinds of internal checks, could in a measure compensate for the lack of virtue in the people, not by attempting to reform them, but by creating a mechanism which would neutralize selfishness.

This picture may seem a little unsettling at first, because it is not pleasing to learn that the aim of the framers of the United States Constitution was to separate virtue from government, to make virtue less essential. But what is the alternative? Would one want a government whose successful operation depended on the goodness of rulers, where there were no checks to prevent their selfishness from oppressing the people? Of course not. All want a government that weeds out the evil desires of men as far as possible and which, in bringing about good, serves the public as a whole rather than private interests. Only an instrument that does not depend upon the virtue of the people or even the virtue of the legislature can do the job.

The opposite extreme, however, is dangerous. We cannot disregard the importance of virtue in society and in government just because the Constitution provides a mechanism for sifting out selfishness and checking the lust for power. In the nation as a whole, but hopefully not in the Church, there is a tendency to neglect the importance of the virtue of the American people and to fail to recognize what a valuable and critical resource it is. But the Constitution does not provide a fail-safe system. Malevolence is not always detected and punished. Watergate has to some extent reassured us that even a president with malicious aims can somehow be checked, but Watergate would never have turned out favorably were it not for virtue somewhere among government leaders. Mormons above all others should recognize that virtue is absolutely essential to the well-being of the United States.

The significance of virtue is best understood scripturally through study of the passages on the Constitution in the Doctrine and Covenants in the light of related passages in the Book of Mormon. The key section is Mosiah 29, where King Mosiah abdicated the throne and effected a constitutional change in Nephite government. Kings had governed Nephites up to this point. The first Nephi was made a king by his people, and his successors at the head of the government were called second Nephi, third Nephi, etc., like George the first, George the second, and George the third. When groups separated from the Nephite population, the people would choose a king from among themselves. What is unusual about the Book of Mormon in American terms, though not unusual in Biblical terms, is that the Book of Mormon kings did not desire to be monarchs. Nephi at first refused, as did Mosiah. Alma the Elder, the leader of the group that was baptized in the Waters of Mormon, absolutely refused. Eventually the younger Mosiah, when faced with the problems in the succession, proposed that kingship be abolished altogether and judgeships established instead. A strange incident: a monarch abdicates and abolishes his monarchy.

The change brought about by the people of Mosiah when they chose judges instead of a king brings us closer to an understanding of our modern constitution. The chief judges served for life: they were not reelected every year, and for the most part the office was hereditary. The son of the chief judge had a right to the chief judgeship, and so it was handed down from father to son. They were initially elected by the voice of the people, but so were the kings. In terms of how they achieved office, the tenure of office, and succession, a chief judge resembled a king. Chief judgeships were not democracies. There was no legislature, for example. The people voted on major constitutional issues but not on the everyday affairs of government, and no elections to office are recorded in the Book of Mormon after this first election. If there were elections, they were not deemed important enough to be entered into the record.

What, then, was the difference between the chief judges and the king? The difference lay in what was identified by Mosiah as the evils of kingship, which arose from a power which the king possessed and the chief judge did not. The king was sovereign; the chief judge was not. As such, the king had the highest conceivable power of government, the power to make laws. The evil of a king, Mosiah said, was that a corrupt king had the power to make corrupt laws. The people were then led into evil by the laws, evil for which they were not responsible. Thus one man corrupted the whole culture, and those living under the evil king did not have the agency to choose between good and evil.

A good king like Mosiah avoided the problem apparently by making no laws at all. Mosiah governed only according to the law of God, handed down from generations. The advantage of a judge was that he lacked the power to make laws. He was not a sovereign, and so was restricted to delivering judgments according to the law of God. The chief grounds for impeaching a chief judge was an attempt to judge according to some law other than the law of God. Thus, under judgeships, God made the laws and was sovereign.

The advantage of this form of government was that the people were responsible for their own sins. They were not compelled by an evil king to perform acts contrary to their consciences and to the will of the Lord. They had their agency:

> And I command you to do these things . . . and that ye have no king; that if these people commit sins and iniquities they shall be answered upon their own heads.
>
> For behold I say unto you, the sins of many people have been caused by the iniquities of their kings; therefore their iniquities are answered upon the heads of their kings. (Mosiah 29:30–31)

Mosiah called the condition of the people under judgeships "equality," by which he meant equality of responsibility. One man alone was not responsible for the righteousness of the nation. Each man was responsible for himself.

After hearing from Mosiah, his people were convinced of the truth of his words. "They relinquished their desires for a king, and became exceedingly anxious that every man should have an equal chance throughout all the land; yea, and every man expressed a willingness to answer for his own sins" (Mosiah 29:38). Strange as it may seem today, the Nephite people were pleased that they were to be held responsible for their own sins.[4]

Mosiah's definition of equality as equality of responsibility is significant because it bears on the interpretation of our Constitution. When the Lord endorsed the Constitution of the United States, he proclaimed that under the Constitution "every man may act in doctrine and principle pertaining to futurity, according to the moral agency which I have given unto him, that every man may be accountable for his own sins in the day of judgment" (D&C 101:78). The Constitution has the same effect today as judgeships in Mosiah's time: it preserves the agency of the people and makes each man accountable for his own sins. Judging from the Lord's words in these two instances, this is an eternal principle.

How does this apply to America today? The important point is that America is not now under the law of God, as were the people under judgeships in Mosiah's time. Americans still have a human sovereign with law-making power over them. Sovereignty has passed from the king to the people, and with it the power to make laws. The representatives of the people in the United States have the legislative power of a king. There is safety in this arrangement, because it is harder to corrupt a whole people than to corrupt a king. But it is just possible that Americans may be living on one of those boundaries in human history when the virtue of an entire nation is in jeopardy, when the will of the whole people is approaching the point where it desires evil, and laws could be made which would compel men to do evil as the wicked kings in the Book of Mormon did. As religious faith deteriorates and moral standards inevitably fall, total corruption is possible.

To be subject to a sovereign people which is corrupt and vicious is a more terrible situation than to be subject to a corrupt monarch. The recourse under a corrupt monarch is revolution, but what is the recourse under a corrupt democracy? A people cannot revolt against itself. Mosiah told his people what must happen: "And if the time comes that the voice of the people doth choose iniquity, then is the time that the judgments of God will come upon you; yea, then is the time he will visit you with great destruction even as he has hitherto visited this land" (Mosiah 29:27). The entire society must be dismantled as it was in the days of Noah.

I do not think America's condition is hopeless; an alliance in the cause of virtue is still possible. By linking arms with all those who believe in God or adhere to high moral standards, the Saints can help preserve the Constitution and free agency. But it is more important still to nourish the ground from which these men and women of America spring, that ground of faith and conviction from which virtue ultimately grows. The highest kind of political activity, then, is to teach virtue and faith. Ultimately there is no other way to preserve the Constitution of the United States and the freedom which it was established to protect. Citizens of the United States claiming Latter-day Saint heritage are required to act decisively to strengthen the moral foundations of liberty, that "every man may act in doctrine and principle pertaining to futurity, according to the moral agency" which the Lord has given him.

This work cannot be undertaken successfully in the last hour. The last hour is too late.

1. Gordon S. Wood, *The Creation of the American Republic, 1776–1787*, Institute of Early American History and Culture (Chapel Hill, N.C.: University of North Carolina Press, 1969).

2. Braintree, 8 January 1776, *Warren-Adams Letters, Being Chiefly a Correspondence Among John Adams, Samuel Adams, and James Warren*, vol. 72, Massachusetts Historical Society, *Collections* (Boston, 1917), p. 202.

3. John Jay to Washington, Philadelphia, 27 June 1786; and Washington to John Jay, Mount Vernon, 1 August 1786, in Samuel Eliot Morison, ed., *Sources and Documents Illustrating the American Revolution, 1764–1788, and the Formation of the Federal Constitution*, 2nd ed. (London: Oxford University Press, 1929), pp. 214, 216.

4. For a further explication of the themes in the preceding paragraph, see Richard L. Bushman, "The Book of Mormon and the American Revolution," to appear in a forthcoming volume of essays in honor of Hugh Nibley to be published by Brigham Young University Press.

J. Reuben Clark, Jr.:
The Constitution
and the Great
Fundamentals*

Martin B. Hickman, *professor of political science and dean of the College of Social Sciences at Brigham Young University, says that J. Reuben Clark, Jr.'s, commentary on the Constitution is set apart from most Mormon commentary because of his "careful, precise, and full statement of the historical, philosophical, and scriptural basis of his convictions." Hickman focuses on three aspects of Clark's commentaries on the Constitution: his belief that it was an inspired document, his insistence on the centrality of the separation of powers, and his devotion to the First Amendment. He concludes with a statement of Clark's belief in the great fundamentals of the Constitution.*

Dean Hickman received his Ph.D. at the University of Utah and had one year of postdoctoral work at Harvard. He was with the U.S. Foreign Service and was on the faculty of the University of Southern California before he joined the faculty at Brigham Young University. In addition to his administrative duties as dean of the College of Social Sciences, he teaches constitutional law.

*Reprinted from *Brigham Young University Studies* (Spring 1973) by permission of the author and publisher; copyright 1973 by Brigham Young University Press.

THE ASSERTION THAT THE Constitution of the United States is an inspired document made so frequently by Mormon writers and speakers is rarely probed for its full meaning; generally, they are content to deal with the question rhetorically rather than analytically. The most important exception to this rule, at least among Church leaders, was J. Reuben Clark, Jr.

President Clark is set apart from most Mormon commentators on the Constitution by three distinctive characteristics. The first is the eloquence of his exposition and defense of the Constitution as a political document. His sure rhetorical ear rarely fails him as he searches for the right word, the pungent phrase, or the stirring sentence or paragraph as he presses his case on the reader. As has been said elsewhere, what sets him apart from other Mormon commentators on the Constitution is not primarily his views but "the felicity with which he expressed them, the intensity with which he held them and the persistence with which he repeated them."[1]

Secondly, President Clark's writings, lectures, and sermons on the Constitution contain, when taken as a whole, a careful, precise, and full statement of the historical, philosophical, and scriptural basis of his convictions. He thus welded cogent analytical arguments for fundamental constitutional principles to the spiritual insights provided by the scriptures. Both elements are important to his constitutional thought; each might stand readily alone, but they are mutually reinforced by the skillful and eloquent statement President Clark gives them.

Lastly, President Clark brought to his consideration of the American Constitution a deep sense of history. In his view, "the Constitution was born, not only of the wisdom and experience of the generation that wrought it, but also out of the wisdom of the long generations that had gone before and which had been transmitted to them through tradition and the pages of history."[2] The framers, he carefully pointed out, not only understood the meaning of the legacy which history and tradition had bequeathed them, but coupled that knowledge to their own colonial experience so that when it came to political questions they were at home not only in Virginia, Maryland, or New York, but also "equally at home in Rome, in Athens, in Paris, and in London."[3]

It was precisely because President Clark understood the importance and relevance of history that he could appreciate and emphasize the meaningful way in which the Founding Fathers drew simultaneously on their experience and historical knowledge to write a document whose relevance reached both forward and backward across time.

A complete study of President Clark's commentary on the Constitution would require an entire monograph, so all that can be undertaken in a relatively short article is an examination of some aspects of that commentary. Three aspects of President Clark's commentaries on the Constitution stand out: (1) his belief that it was an inspired document; (2) his insistence on the centrality of the separation of powers; and (3) his devotion to the freedoms enshrined in the First Amendment. In view of the salience of these points in President Clark's constitutional thought, they will be the focus of the balance of this paper.

History and Inspiration

President Clark, of course, does not stand alone in his belief that the Constitution was an inspired document. Joseph Smith, Brigham Young, and other presidents of the Church taught the same, and ultimately they all drew on the Doctrine and Covenants for justification of their belief. Interestingly, the Doctrine and Covenants does not contain the phrase "inspired document," but that phrase is by no means an unjustified paraphrase of the passages in the Doctrine and Covenants. What the Doctrine and Covenants does assert is that the Lord "established the Constitution of this land, by the hands of wise men whom I raised up unto this very purpose" (see D&C 101:77–80). Drawing on this declaration, Mormon commentators from the beginning of the Church have insisted on the primacy of the Constitution as a model for human government. President Clark constantly underlined the importance of this tradition in Mormon life. "From the time I stood at my mother's knee," he told a group of bankers in 1938, "I have been taught to reverence the Constitution as God-given."[4] That parental teaching—reinforced by modern scripture—shaped all of President Clark's thinking about the Constitution. But he saw the Constitution in its broadest possible application. It was for him not simply the form of government best suited to the needs of a new nation struggling to free itself from the coils of colonialism, but also a document containing principles which were applicable everywhere. It was his firm belief that: "In broad outline the Lord has declared through our Constitution his form for human government."[5] He repeated that belief in so many ways, on so many different occasions, across so many years, that there can be little doubt about the importance it played in his life. Furthermore, it is the constant background against which his constitutional writings must be assessed.

What is unique about President Clark's belief in the Constitution as an inspired document is the way he links that faith to an understanding of history. There is nothing in President Clark's writings on the Constitution which suggests that he thought the whole of the drama of the Constitution was played in Philadelphia in 1787. Rather, he saw the Constitution as emerging from a long historical process. He assessed the framers of the Constitution as being men of great historical knowledge as well as practical experience. In the same vein, President Clark was fully aware that the political principles which are enshrined in the Constitution had their origins in the development of Anglo-Saxon legal and political experience. The Common Law, and English constitutional experience, were the schoolmasters of the framers: "They remembered the Barons and King John at Runnymede. They were thoroughly indoctrinated in the principle that the true sovereignty rested in the people."[6] They brought to their task, as he clearly saw, a mastery of the political ideas which had gradually emerged from the long struggle of Englishmen for self-government.

While President Clark's sense of history led him to see the relevance of the past to the emergence of the Constitution, he did not survey history with the naturalistic eyes of the secular historian. Rather, he viewed history through the lens of faith, and for him the Constitution was simultaneously a beginning and an end. As an end, it was the culmination of the effort to find the political framework for assuring the continued development and protection of human freedom. As a beginning it marked the birth of the "first new nation" which had shed the unwanted baggage of the past, while taking from the past the best of its lessons.

This beginning and end were for President Clark not the haphazard results of historical chance, but rather the manifestations of the divine will in the affairs of men. For him, the whole of the Anglo-Saxon political and legal tradition was part of the "establishment" process which resulted in the American Constitution. It was his conception of history as a seamless web which enabled him to maintain his religious faith in the Constitution as an inspired document while judging clearly how much it owed to the past. After reading President Clark on the Constitution, no one can believe that the framers created something out of nothing, for he shows how heavily they drew upon history and their own experience in writing the Constitution. But likewise no one can come from a study of President Clark's writings on the Constitution without being touched by his testimony that while they came to their task, "rich in intellectual endowment and ripened in experience," they were after all "in God's hands; he guided them in their epoch making deliberations in Independence Hall."[7]

Separation of Powers

At the heart of President Clark's defense of the Constitution was his insistence on the necessity of the separation of powers. In his view the Founding Fathers had created a government in which the three branches of government—executive, legislative, and judicial—were "wholly independent of [each] other. No one of them might encroach upon the other. No one of them might delegate its power to another."[8] He asserted, with the Founding Fathers, that the accumulation of all governmental powers in the same hands was the very definition of tyranny. Any changes which tended to erode that separation had to be resisted vigorously.

President Clark's defense of the separation of powers as the central idea of the Constitution went far beyond a mere assertion that such separation was a protection against tyranny, and beyond a repetition of quotes from the Founding Fathers. He carefully spelled out his own understanding of the difference that doctrine had made in the political development of England and the English colonies compared to that of continental Europe.[9] That comparative study led him to contrast the way in which the legacy of the Roman Empire, and particularly the Roman civil law, had provided justification for the absolute monarchies of continental Europe, while in England the monarchy was being increasingly subjected to the will of the people. Those simultaneous developments, he argued, were related to fundamental ideas about the nature of law. While the governing principle on the Continent inherited from Roman law was that the will of the emperor was law, that will knew no bounds but the emperor's adherence to traditions or his sense of morality.[10] If the emperor lacked these restraining virtues, there was nothing that he might not will into law. For the emperor to have this power it was, of course, necessary for him to possess legislative and judicial as well as executive power. President Clark saw a relation between this concentration of all governmental power in the same hands and the absence of liberty on the Continent. The peoples of western and southern Europe, he wrote,

> have lived under this concept (sometimes more, sometimes less), and, when the concept has been operative, have suffered the resulting trage-dies—loss of liberty, oppression, great poverty among the masses, insecurity, wanton disregard of human life, and a host of the relatives of these evil broods.[11]

Furthermore, he believed that the civil law had left another unfortunate legacy to the people of Europe. The very nature of the civil law, with its justification resting in the will of the emperor and its codification into the great codes of Justinian and Theodosius, dictated a system under which "the people look into the law to see what they may do."[12] This meant, of course, that these governments were governments of residual powers; that is, they had all power unless they chose not to exercise a specific power. Despite a long literary tradition in Europe which made kings subject to the will of God, to natural law, or in some cases to contracts with the subjects, the political realities made rebellion the only effective way of enforcing these limitations on royal rulers. "The rigors of this system," President Clark pointed out, "were at times mitigated by a benign sovereign, but only to the extent that he desired."[13] Attempts to restrict the royal will by legislative bodies were thwarted by the fact that they existed at the sovereign's pleasure, and "any attempt by those bodies to go contrary to his will was somehow made ineffective; sometimes such efforts were treasonable and so treated."[14]

This royal domination of the governmental process and the liberties of the people does not mean that men were not governed by law. What it does mean is that men were not governed by laws of their own making. The rule of law had a restricted meaning in such a system. It meant that the sovereign ought to be bound by the law just as his subjects were. It did not mean that there were some laws which the sovereign could not change, or that there were some rights of his subjects which he could not violate. The consequences of such a system were to limit the development of political and civil liberties to a very restricted sphere and to hold the nations of western Europe far behind the development of England in the ways in which the people were able to subject the government and the monarchy to their will.

In contrast to the continental system, President Clark argued, political development in England had resulted in the will of the sovereign being brought under the control of the people. The Glorious Revolution of 1688 had fixed once and for all in English constitutional development the concept that the sovereign owed his rightful possession of the throne to the will of Parliament, and that Parliament was responsible solely to the people. In addition to this development of parliamentary control over the king, there had emerged over a long period of time the notion that there were some things which the executive could not do without legislative authority. This notion had centered principally around the struggle for the power of the purse, and the right of Englishmen not to be taxed unless they were represented in Parliament had become a cherished English right. This principle, President Clark thought, was important not only because it gave the people control over the way in which the government sought to tax their property, but also because it was the foundation of the notion that there were some things which the government could not do unless it was expressly permitted to do so by the elective representatives of the government. It was from this point only a short distance to the idea of a written constitution which specified certain governmental powers which might be exercised by the government, but specifying others which should be denied the government under any circumstances.

In this context the idea of the rule of law takes on an expanded meaning. Not only does the rule of law mean that the sovereign is bound by the law and must live under the law as do his subjects, but it also means that, as President Clark pointed out: "The people specifically grant to their government the powers and the authorities which they wish their government to have. When any power is exercised that is not granted, it is usurpation."[15] This concept of "limited government" is the fundamental premise on which the American constitutional system is based. However, the notion of a limited government is so familiar to most Americans that it is easy to forget how long and difficult its establishment has been. Moreover, it is easy to assume that it has held sway in all parts of the world and that somehow all civilized states are based on the same fundamental notions. President Clark wished clearly to point out that what had happened in the Constitutional Convention, and in the ratification process which followed that convention, was a new departure in the history of the world.[16] It not only brought into American government the notion of limited government which had emerged in England, but it added to that notion the idea of a written constitution which specifically spelled out the rights and liberties of the people which would be immune to governmental interference. In the establishment of a government based on a written document, President Clark saw the culmination of a long historical process which had its beginnings deep in the efforts of the English people to free themselves from the tyranny of absolute monarchy.

The crucial development in the emergence of the concept of limited government was the introduction of the doctrine of the separation of powers in English constitutional discourse during the English Civil War. The notion that the executive and legislative powers ought to be separated was first introduced to oppose the practice of the House of Commons of trying judicial cases. The intent was to "assure that accused persons be tried by the known procedures of courts of justice and convicted by settled rules previously enacted, rather than according to the considerations of policy which moved legislative bodies."[17] But soon a second and potentially more vital argument entered the debate. A major function of Parliament was thought by Englishmen of the period to be the supervision of the administration of the law. If Parliament were simultaneously charged with the task of exacting general rules and supervising the application of the rules in particular cases, then, as a John Lilburne argued as early as 1649, Englishmen would be a nation of fools. For if Parliament could "execute the law, they might do palpable injustice, and maladminister it";[18] but in that case to whom could those so wronged turn for justice? Surely not to Parliament, for would not the members of Parliament turn to this accuser "to vote that man a traitor and destroy him"?[19]

Support for the separation of powers as the cornerstone of limited government spread rapidly in the period after the English Civil War. John Locke and Montesquieu included a version of the concept in their political writings, and by 1787, when the Founding Fathers began the task of writing the Constitution, it was firmly fixed as one of the brightest stars in their political firmament. It was, as President Clark pointed out, because they were "aware that a combination of legislative, executive and judicial power in one person or body was destructive of all freedom and justice" that they wrote a constitution providing for "a government in which these three branches [judicial, executive, legislative] were distinct and wholly independent the one from the other."[20]

President Clark's assertion that the three branches of government were wholly independent of each other must not be taken to mean that he was unaware of the implications of the system of checks and balances which coexists in the Constitution with separation of powers. They are, after all, two different principles. The separation of powers, the Founding Fathers knew from their English heritage, was a necessary concomitant of the generality and prospectivity of law, for only where the powers of government were separate were the conditions created which assured that general and prospective laws would be maintained. The same English heritage had also taught them that a separation of powers was not likely to last unless some barriers were created to prevent the flow of power to the legislative branch. Of course, the idea of checks and balances was not a new one. Polybius had described the Roman constitution in terms of checks and balances; but this device was used in Rome not to maintain the balance between the branches of government, but to balance the power of contending social classes by giving each class representation in a separate political institution. It was Thomas Jefferson who, on the basis of his knowledge of English constitutional development and as a result of his Virginia experience, first saw that unless some way were found to maintain a separation of powers, all power would gradually flow to the legislative branch; just as in the English constitutional development, Parliament, through its power of the purse, had slowly but surely gathered all power into its hands.[21] Jefferson, therefore, argued that a system of checks and balances should be adopted to assure the continued separation of powers among the three branches of government.

Also, the authors of *The Federalist* noted that the "great security against a gradual concentration of the several powers in the same department, consists in giving to those who administer each department the necessary constitutional means and personal motives to resist encroachments of the others."[22] They rejected the argument that such formal arrangements were unnecessary to protect freedom. For, as they wrote, "dependence on the people is, no doubt, the primary control on the government; but experience has taught mankind the necessity of auxiliary precautions."[23]

President Clark clearly knew all of this. He understood the ways in which the branches of government check each other. He knew that the right of the president to suggest legislation, or to veto legislation which he thought unwise, made him part of the legislative process. He understood the legal and political implications of the practice of judicial review. What he insisted upon was the independence of the branches in their assigned constitutional spheres. He was opposed to "court packing," to congressional subservience to presidential demands, and to presidential usurpation of congressional prerogatives. These all took, he believed, the American government back down the path of political repression which the framers had so carefully sought to avoid. His insistence on the necessity of the "complete" independence of each branch of government was, therefore, made with a full knowledge that the Constitution itself provided for their interdependence in certain precise ways. President Clark not only understood this relationship, but thought it to be the genius of the Constitution.

> It is this union of independence and dependence of these branches—legislative, executive and judicial—and of the governmental functions possessed by each of them, that constitutes the marvelous genius of this unrivalled document. The framers had no direct guide in this work, no historical governmental precedent upon which to rely. As I see it, it was here that the divine inspiration came. It was truly a miracle.[24]

President Clark was anxious that such a hard-won victory for the forces of freedom and civil liberty should not be given away unwittingly. He made special efforts, therefore, to call attention to the dangers involved in permitting either of the three branches of government to usurp powers which did not rightfully belong to them. One of the issues to which he addressed himself most directly was the question of whether there exists under the American Constitution a set of war powers which the president could exercise in time of war that were separate and distinct from the president's executive power.[25] President Clark argued cogently that the plain words of the Constitution granted the war powers specifically to Congress. These included the power to declare war and to provide for its prosecution by appropriating monies for the armed forces and drafting men into the armed services. Furthermore, he pointed out, the framers intended that such be the case. The president's right to act in times of war, he argued, existed only where Congress undertook to provide him with power under its constitutional authority to make and declare war. President Clark was also aware that the president might take the necessary action to repel an invasion, or that in times of war Congress had full power to give the president powers of "the widest scope, including provisions derogatory and even largely destructive of the ordinary peace-time civil rights of individuals."[26]

Although President Clark did not live to see our day, one cannot help but feel that he would have been most disturbed by the pursuance of a large-scale war in Vietnam without a declaration of war by Congress.[27] At the same time, one cannot help but feel that he would have been scornful of the outcries of many politicians and legislators about the usurpation of legislative authority inherent in the conduct of major hostilities without congressional authority. He might have justifiably pointed out to them that had they heeded his words of warning about the growing excesses of executive power in the mid-thirties and forties they would not have had to deal with presidents who were able to conduct a war of considerable magnitude without congressional authority. He might also have pointed out to them that had the Congress been jealous of its constitutional prerogatives and rights, had it maintained its constitutional freedom of action, and not, in many respects, become the handmaiden of the executive branch, Congress would have been in a better position to enforce upon the president a limitation in his conduct of the war.

Limited Government

The tradition of limited government which President Clark found so intimately connected with the principle of separation of powers found expression in the American Constitution, he thought, in still other ways. The most important of these were the limitations on governmental power explicitly placed in the Constitution by the framers. One might note that two of these limitations are rather routinely overlooked by commentators on the Constitution, but they are important in the maintenance of the principle of a separation of powers. The first is the prohibition against *ex post facto* laws. It is clear that if law is to be meaningful it must not be capricious, and it can be prevented from being capricious only when it is prospective, that is, when it applies in the future and not in the past. Therefore, the framers of the Constitution prohibited Congress from passing *ex post facto* laws, thus ensuring that citizens would not be punished for acts which were legal when they were undertaken. Another prohibition in the Constitution central to the question of the separation of powers is a prohibition against bills of attainder. Bills of attainder are legislative declarations of guilt, the issuance of which, under the separation of powers, must be left to the courts since the role of Congress or the legislature is simply to declare the general law. The question of whether any individual falls within the purview of that law or is guilty under the terms of its sanctions is a question for the courts; if the legislature could declare who is guilty under the terms of the general law, it would thereby gain all power over the citizens in its own hands. Consequently, to preserve the separation of powers, the framers of the Constitution very wisely banned those two ancient enemies of the rule of law—*ex post facto* laws and bills of attainder.

At the same time that the founders were writing into the Constitution the provisions banning bills of attainder and *ex post facto* laws, they did not find it necessary to enact a specific bill of rights.[28] The prevailing opinion in the Constitutional Convention was that a bill of rights was unnecessary since it was clearly understood that the new government would be a government of delegated powers and could therefore exercise only those powers which were expressly given to it by the Constitution. All other rights of citizens were automatically outside the purview of the federal government. In the ensuing debates over ratification it became clear that it would be difficult to obtain the ratifications of the new constitution unless a bill of rights was specifically included. Therefore, several amendments were drawn up with the promise that they would be submitted to the states for ratification as soon as possible after the new government had come into power. Because this was done, the Bill of Rights, which is at the core of the protection of our civil liberties today, was not adopted as a part of the Constitution at the convention.

President Clark was fully aware of the way in which the Bill of Rights had entered the Constitution. Yet, it was his firm belief that the Bill of Rights, no less than the body of the Constitution, fell within the definition of being divinely inspired. He bore his testimony in the April conference of 1957 that the "Constitution of the United States as it came from the hands of the framers, with its coterminous Bill of Rights," was an integral part of his religious faith. "It is," he said, "A revelation from the Lord. I believe and reverence its God-inspired provisions."[29] Since for President Clark the whole concept of limited government was a divinely inspired idea, it is only logical that he should believe that the Bill of Rights, which is the concrete manifestation of that tradition, should warrant the title of "inspired."

Central to the concept of limited government, and in President Clark's eyes, no less important than the separation of powers, was the doctrine represented by the Bill of Rights that there are some areas of human life in which the government has no right to interfere. This concept assumes that the individual is morally supreme and that his moral life can never be invaded by the state. This moral life finds its expression in the exchange of ideas and in the exercise of religion. Therefore, it is in these realms of human existence that the conflict between the state and the individual is the sharpest. Moreover, it is precisely in his moral life that the state seeks to restrict the individual, because it is the individual's claim to moral supremacy which undermines the state's demands that its existence is a transcendent end to which the rights of the individual must be subordinated. In the late thirties, President Clark put the matter squarely when he observed that "the great struggle which now rocks the whole earth more and more takes on the character of a struggle of the individual versus the State."[30] He went on to ask: "Does the individual exist for the benefit of the State, or does the State exist for the benefit of the individual?"[31] There is no doubt, of course, where President Clark stood on the matter, since the whole of his political and religious philosophy rested on the notion of the moral supremacy of the individual.

It is precisely because he was so concerned with the moral supremacy of the individual and the preservation of individual rights against government interference that he saw in the Bill of Rights a great monument to the progress which the human spirit had made in its search for freedom. He was particularly concerned with the protection of the freedoms guaranteed by the First Amendment: freedom of the press, of speech, and of religion.

His defense of the freedoms of the First Amendment was made at two levels. The first was a general assertion of the necessity to protect the rights of all men against the dictates of the state. At that level he was concerned with the necessity for freedom of the press and of speech as a way of maintaining responsible government. He pointed out that the Founding Fathers had had considerable experience with attempts to control what they had written and spoken in criticism of the government, and they knew, in his pungent phrase, "how tyranny and oppression smart."[32] He was also impressed by the way that they understood how government officials are prone to resent any criticism and to take whatever action they can to suppress that criticism. It was President Clark's opinion that the Founding Fathers had never intended that the means of communication and publicity should be regulated so as to eliminate criticism of governmental policy or employees. "The fathers felt that when they protected freedom of speech and of the press against governmental interference," he wrote, "they had effectively guaranteed the citizens' freedom to talk and write as they felt and thought about their own government."[33] President Clark said clearly that without the existence of a free press, and without the right of individuals to speak freely about the way their government was being operated, the chances of freedom being maintained were reduced.

Coupled with President Clark's belief in the necessity of freedom of speech and of the press if government were to remain limited was his equally fervent belief that government had no right to interfere in the religious life of its citizens. In 1938, he commented on the tendency then extant in the world, and which has certainly multiplied many times over in our day, for governments to restrict freedom of religion—what he called "the holy of holies of the soul of man."[34] He was outraged that the state should intrude onto such sacred ground and there seek to dethrone God and exalt the state into God's place. "This is the archest treason of them all. For man robbed of God becomes a brute."[35] President Clark was explicit in his belief that for a government to trespass on the religious life of its citizens was a sin of the highest magnitude. "This sin," he said in a sentence of prophetic majesty in its condemnation of evil, "must be felt, not told, for words cannot measure the height and breadth of this iniquity; nor can human mind encompass the punishment of those who shall commit this sin."[36]

At a second level, President Clark was particularly concerned that Latter-day Saints should give full support to the constitutional freedoms of religion and speech provided by the Constitution. He recalled to their memory the trials and persecution which the Mormon people had suffered; and he reminded them, in the April conference of 1935, that they needed the Constitution and its "guarantees of liberty and freedom more than any other people in the world, for, weak and few as we are, we stand naked and helpless except when clothed with its benign provisions."[37] He told his audience that nothing was so important to the Mormon people as "this guarantee of religious freedom, because underneath and behind all that lies in our lives, all that we do in our lives, is our religion, our worship, our belief and faith in God."[38] That call to support the constitutional liberties seems to be as urgent and valid today as it was in 1935, and indeed President Clark returned to the theme in a conference speech in 1957 in which he said: "Our own prophets have declared in our day the responsibility of the Elders of Zion in the preservation of the Constitution. We cannot, guiltless, escape that responsibility. We cannot be laggards, nor can we be deserters."[39]

One is impressed, upon reading the writings of President Clark on the Constitution, to see how faithfully he stays with the fundamentals. It is the separation of powers and its intimate relationship with the development of limited government which occupy so much of his concern; it is the Bill of Rights with its limitations on the power of government to interfere with the moral life of man with which he is so impressed. This concern for fundamentals makes him aware that some aspects of the Constitution do not warrant the same divine approval as do these great fundamentals. As he told a group of bankers: "It is not my belief nor is it the doctrine of my Church that the Constitution is a fully grown document. On the contrary, we believe it must grow and develop to meet the changing needs of an advancing world."[40] It was clear, he told the group, that given the lust of men for power and gain it was inevitable that legislation must be constantly adjusted to take into account the never-ending problems which human nature presents. But, he insisted, "all such changes must be made to protect and preserve our liberties, not to take them from us. Greater freedom, not slavery, must follow every constitutional change."[41] President Clark was concerned, however, that constitutional change might come, and had come, not by the prescribed methods spelled out in the Constitution, but in the urgency of a crisis by a careless disregard for constitutional principles. He was concerned that the American people might acquiesce in constitutional changes which appeared to satisfy the demands of the moment, but which in the long run would not produce the increase of freedom by which he thought each constitutional change should be judged. His was a consistent reminder, therefore, that the American people, and particularly the Mormon community, must look to the fundamentals of the Constitution, must constantly review the purposes for which the Constitution was written, must be aware of the struggles out of which the Constitution emerged, and that they must remember the Founding Fathers' hope that their posterity might be spared the burden of repressive government—a burden they knew only too well. If the American people, he thought, could focus upon the fundamentals of the Constitution, and if they could remember that they cannot safely abrogate the great principles on which the Constitution rests without risking their freedom and that of their children, then there might be hope for the future.

Thus President Clark's understanding of the dynamics of human life, and the ways in which new problems constantly confront those who are called to govern the affairs of men, was simultaneously a recognition of the need for change and an increasing awareness of the continuing relevance of the great fundamentals of the Constitution. It was his own belief, he told that group of bankers in 1938, and the belief of the Mormon people,

> that in all that relates to its great fundamentals—in the division of powers and their full independence one from the other, in the equal administration of the laws, in the even-handed dispensing of justice, in the absence of all class and casts [sic], in the freedom of the press and of speech and of religion—we believe that in all such matters as these our Constitution must not be changed.[42]

It was the defense of the great fundamentals which concerned President Clark over a lifetime of devotion to a Constitution which he believed to be divinely inspired. He believed in the ultimate triumph of the fundamental principles of the Constitution, but his vision of that triumph discloses the heart of a great American whose summons is not that of the chauvinistic flag waver but of the true patriot who sees with clarity the true mission of America.

> Gentlemen, do you not catch a vision of this glory of America, not the glory of a conquest bought with our blood, of a conquest over a torn, maimed, and hating foe, of a conquest that however it may seem, yet nevertheless always leaves the world poorer and more wretched, with more of woe and misery and sin and despair and hate and damnation than before it came;—not of these conquests.
>
> But the conquest of peace and joy, the conquest of bringing more to eat and more to wear, of bringing more comfort, more education, more culture, the conquest of liberty over tyranny that all men may know and have the free institutions which are ours, the conquest of caste and legalized privilege and of all social inequalities, the conquest of want and misery, of hunger, and nakedness, a conquest of war itself, so that peace and "righteousness shall cover the earth as the waters cover the mighty deep," a conquest that shall bring a true millennium.[43]

1. Martin B. Hickman and Ray C. Hillam, "J. Reuben Clark, Jr.: Political Isolationism Revisited," *Dialogue* 7 (Spring 1972):39.

2. *Church News*, 29 November 1952, p. 3.

3. J. Reuben Clark, Jr. in *Conference Report*, April 1957, p. 48.

4. "Constitutional Government: Our Birthright Threatened," *Vital Speeches of the Day*, 1 January 1939, p. 177.

5. *Conference Report*, April 1957, p. 52.

6. *Church News*, 29 November 1952, p. 12.

7. *Conference Report*, April 1957, p. 48.

8. *Church News*, 29 November 1952, p. 12.

9. President Clark's article in the *Church News*, cited above, spells out his view on this comparison in some detail.

10. Francis D. Wormuth, *The Origins of Modern Constitutionalism* (New York: Harper & Brothers, 1949), p. 29. Professor Wormuth points out that the concept current in the medieval world that the sovereign must obey the laws of God and nature was not drawn from Roman law, "for the Roman jurists were clear that any imperial command, however unreasonable, was law."

11. *Church News*, 29 November 1952, p. 12.

12. Ibid.

13. Ibid.

14. Ibid.

15. "Constitutional Government," p. 175.

16. *Church News*, 29 November 1952, p. 12.

17. Wormuth, *Modern Constitutionalism*, p. 64.

18. Ibid., p. 66.

19. Ibid. On the development of the theory and meaning of the separation of powers, see W. B. Gwyn, *The Meaning of the Separation of Powers* (The Hague: Martinus Nijhoff, 1966). Gwyn deals rather more fully with the authors who have written on the separation of powers than does Wormuth, but he follows him rather carefully on the issues discussed in this paper.

20. "Constitutional Government," p. 176.

21. Phillip S. Foner, ed., *Basic Writings of Thomas Jefferson* (New York: Wiley Book Company, 1944). Jefferson described the Virginia experience with a constitution which provided for a separation of powers, but which omitted checks and balances, in the following passage: "The judiciary and the executive members were left dependent on the legislature for subsist-

ence in office, and some of them for their continuance in it. If, therefore, the legislature assumes executive and judiciary powers, no opposition is likely to be made; nor, if made, can be effectual; because in that case they may put their proceedings into the form of acts of assembly, which will render them obligatory on the other branches. They have accordingly, in many instances decided rights which should have been left to judicial controversy, and the direction of the executive, during the whole time of their session, is becoming habitual and familiar" (Ibid., p. 132).

22. *The Federalist,* No. 51 (New York: Modern Library, 1932), p. 337.

23. Ibid. The arguments for a system of checks and balances to maintain a separation of powers are developed in *The Federalist,* Nos. 47–51.

24. *Church News,* 29 November 1952, p. 12.

25. Ibid., p. 13. For a careful analysis of presidential war powers which lends full support to President Clark's views on this issue, see Francis D. Wormuth, "The Nixon Theory of the War Power: A Critique," *California Law Review* 60, no. 3 (May 1972):623–703.

26. *Church News,* 29 November 1952, p. 13.

27. See his sermon in *Conference Report,* April 1957, pp. 49–50, for a discussion of the war power in which President Clark explains that the framers earnestly sought "to make as nearly as impossible as could be, the malfeasances of the past by men in high executive offices in the future; and seemingly perhaps beyond everything else as a practical matter, to prevent the President from taking us into war of his own volition."

28. Alfred H. Kelley and Winfred A. Harbison, *The American Constitution* (New York: W. W. Norton & Co., 1948), p. 152.

29. *Conference Report,* April 1957, pp. 50–51.

30. "Constitutional Government," p. 174.

31. Ibid.

32. Ibid., p. 176.

33. Ibid.

34. Ibid., p. 175.

35. Ibid.

36. Ibid.

37. *Conference Report,* April 1935, p. 94.

38. Ibid.

39. *Conference Report,* April 1957, p. 52.

40. "Constitutional Government," p. 177.

41. Ibid.

42. Ibid.

43. Ibid., p. 178.

Mormons, the Constitution, and the Host Economy

L. Dwight Israelsen, an economist, maintains that there is a strong sentiment among Mormons in favor of capitalist institutions and attitudes. He argues that capitalism for now best meets the essential criteria of a host economy for Mormonism, and that the Constitution helps guarantee that the conditions of a free economic system will continue to be met. But he concludes that capitalism is transitory for Mormons, since they will eventually turn to a superior economic and political system.

Professor Israelsen received his Ph.D. in economics from the Massachusetts Institute of Technology and is currently on the faculty of the Department of Economics at Brigham Young University, where he teaches comparative economic systems and economic theory.

THERE IS A STRONG SENTIMENT among Mormons today in favor of capitalist institutions and attitudes. This sentiment contrasts sharply with the anti-capitalist tone of official Church pronouncements and policies of the last century, and with the Mormon belief that the communitarian economic system first attempted in the 1830s will eventually be reinstituted. This apparent change in attitudes from the nineteenth to the twentieth centuries has become a major issue in Mormon intellectual history.

In this essay, I review Mormon beliefs about the Constitution and about the ideal economic system in order to develop a pattern or model of behavior against which Mormon economic policies and attitudes may be tested for consistency. First, I describe the economic goals to be achieved in the ideal Christian community and review briefly the various economic institutions employed by Church leaders since 1830. Second, I use Mormon concepts of the inspired Constitution and of the ideal economic system to build the model of Mormon behavior previously mentioned. Finally, I look at several historical examples of Mormon economic policies and attitudes to see whether they are consistent with the model.

The Ideal Economic System

The Mormon Church was organized in 1830. In 1896, Utah was admitted to the Union. The interval between these two events is marked by a series of communitarian and cooperative socioeconomic experiments—the attempts by Joseph Smith and Brigham Young to implement "the more perfect law of the Lord" among the Latter-day Saints. Although the actual institutions varied in organization and in scope, the goal remained the same: to achieve a "oneness" in things temporal and spiritual, an ideal Christian community in which selfishness and greed would be replaced with brotherly love, and competitive capitalism with order and unity.

The blueprint for the ideal community, the law of consecration and stewardship, was announced as early as February 1831 (see D&C 42). The economic goals of the plan included the elimination of poverty, relative economic equality, and group economic self-sufficiency.[1] These goals were to be achieved through the initial "consecration" or deeding of all real and personal property by each Church member to the Presiding Bishop of the Church, and the granting of a "stewardship" or "inheritance" to each family from the consecrated property. Thereafter, there was to be an annual consecration of all surplus production to the "bishop's storehouse."[2]

The consecrations provided an emergency consumption fund and helped finance various investment and religious projects.[3] The socialization of surplus income also ensured continued economic equality by preventing private wealth accumulation. Although the system provided for considerable freedom of enterprise in management and production decisions (limited, of course, by the nature of the stewardship granted), private property rights were not part of the original intent of the plan. The stewardship was a life-lease, conditional on continued faithfulness and subject to revocation by the bishop, who held title to all property.[4]

The communitarian system established by the law of consecration and stewardship operated briefly in 1831 at Thompson, Ohio, and again during 1831–33 in Jackson County, Missouri.[5] A modified form of the law of consecration and stewardship, requiring an initial consecration of surplus property only, followed by annual donation of one-tenth of a member's "increase," was instituted with indifferent success at Far West, Missouri, in 1838.[6] In 1841 the law of tithing was officially adopted by the Church as an admittedly inferior substitute for the "more perfect law of the Lord."[7] The attempts to establish a utopian community in Ohio and Missouri were thwarted by problems involving the legality of the consecration and stewardship deeds, and by lack of support from the Church membership. The final blow was mob violence, which culminated in the death of Joseph Smith in 1844 and the expulsion of the Mormons from the Midwest in 1846.

No attempt was made to reinstitute the law of consecration and stewardship during the Mormons' sojourn in Illinois.[8] However, within a decade of their arrival in the Great Basin, Church members were asked to consecrate their property to Brigham Young as trustee-in-trust for the Church. Although one-third or more of all heads of families in the Utah Territory filed deeds of consecration in the years 1855–58, the Church never did take possession of any property.[9] Problems with the legality of land ownership and transfer in the territory, the arrival of Johnston's Army, and unenthusiastic public response to consecration halted the experiment before it had fairly begun.[10]

In the 1860s, economic cooperation received new emphasis with the establishment of a network of cooperative mercantile and manufacturing enterprises. Not as radical an innovation as the stewardship system, the cooperatives did not require consecration of property, but issued and sold shares of stock and paid dividends. The goals of the experiment included greater unity, increased equality, and self-sufficiency through decreased dependence on "gentile" merchants and increased quantity and assortment of home-produced goods.[11]

The cooperatives were generally successful, sometimes spectacularly so. Model cooperatives were established at Brigham City in 1864, in Spanish Fork, 1867, and in Lehi, 1868. Zion's Cooperative Mercantile Institution, incorporated in 1868, quickly emerged as the territory's most important wholesale store. More than one hundred fifty retail cooperatives and cooperative manufacturing enterprises were established during the late 1860s and early 1870s.[12]

The last quarter of the nineteenth century saw the establishment and abandonment of the United Order of Enoch, the most ambitious Mormon attempt to establish a utopian economic and social system. The completion of the transcontinental railroad in 1869 ended Mormon social and economic isolation and was viewed with some alarm by Church leaders. The large numbers of gentiles flooding into the territory would bring with them all the attitudes and institutions of nineteenth-century American capitalism. The pursuit of profits, concentration of wealth, and competitive individualism which would follow the linkup threatened to seriously erode the bond of selflessness and brotherly love which held together the seams of the Mormon social fabric. Designed to strengthen Mormon resistance to gentile influence and to promote unity in the face of antipolygamy pressures, the united order was Brigham Young's last great effort to build the ideal Christian community.

The first united order was organized in 1874 at St. George, Utah. The last known Church-authorized branch of the order was established in 1893 at Cave Valley, Chihuahua, Mexico. In the intervening years more than two hundred other branches of the united order are known to have been organized in Mormon communities in Utah, Idaho, Wyoming, Nevada, and Arizona, most of them in 1874 and 1875.[13]

Although there was considerable variation in organizational form among the various branches of the united order, nearly all would be classified as producer cooperatives, the exceptions being a few in northern Utah and southern Idaho which were joint-stock companies with significant cooperative characteristics. A producer cooperative is an institution in which workers share the income generated by production, as contrasted to a capitalist firm in which workers are hired at a fixed wage and the owner receives the net income.

The united order producer cooperatives were of two main types: the collective, in which a member's share of income was proportional to the number of hours he worked; and the commune, in which a member's share of income was determined according to need.[14] The great majority of united orders were collectives. The Orderville united order is the best example of the communal type.[15] The communal orders required consecration of all property and labor. The collective orders made the property consecration optional and paid a dividend on property which was consecrated.[16] None of the orders followed the 1831 model of consecration and stewardship.

Although organizationally the United Order of Enoch differed significantly from the communitarian institutions of the 1830s, the goals were nearly identical. They included the elimination of poverty and economic inequality, increases in productivity and income, group economic self-sufficiency, and the elimination of the "ruinous competition," price fluctuations, business cycles, and attitudes of selfishness and greed characteristic of capitalism.[17]

Brigham Young's dream was not to be fulfilled. He died in 1877, barely 3½ years after organizing the first united order; yet he had survived all but a handful of the two hundred branches of the order established before his death.[18] There are many possible reasons for the failure of the movement, including lack of incentives, internal dissension, insufficient capital, the movement toward legal incorporation, the antipolygamy campaign, and the reluctance of the wealthy to put their property in the order. The reasons most often cited by Church leaders were the laziness and the selfishness of the members themselves.[19] The goals were clear, the institutions were available, but the Saints were not ready. In spite of the persecution, the shortages, the losses, and the crop failures, Church leaders from the 1830s to the 1930s (and to the present) insist that the failure to achieve the ideal system is the failure of individuals, not institutions.[20] The change in the nature of the institutions cannot succeed without the change in the nature of man. Man, with God's help, can perfect institutions. With God's help, man, not institutions, must perfect man.

As happened after the failure of the earlier consecration movements, the Mormons in the 1870s and 1880s were provided with institutions more suited to their weaknesses. Zion's Central Board of Trade, which operated from 1878 until 1885, helped provide stable markets and good prices through regulating competition, and it increased private production and employment through a comprehensive resource development plan.[21] The Board of Trade, designed to speed the process of building Zion, succumbed during the antipolygamy raids of the 1880s. Only the "lesser law" of tithing remained to help prepare for that day when the Saints would again be asked to live "the more perfect law of the Lord."

During the last decade of the nineteenth century and during the first part of this century, distinctive Mormon economic institutions were not reintroduced, and Mormons were encouraged to participate in the national economy. The Church readjusted its own business holdings during this period in order to ease the tremendous burden of debt accumulated during the difficult period of the 1880s and 1890s. This inevitably led to business connections with outside sources of capital.

There was one more move toward the "higher law." In response to the Great Depression with its resultant unemployment and poverty, the Church welfare plan was instituted. Incorporating some of the basic principles of the law of consecration and stewardship, the plan provided for the operation of farms and factories by volunteers from local Mormon congregations, with the commodities produced being distributed to the needy through bishops storehouses. This program, much enlarged in scope, continues today, a stepping stone on the path to the "City of God" which Mormons believe must finally be attained.

In summary, then:

1. The major economic goals of the ideal system are economic equality, the elimination of poverty, and group economic self-sufficiency.

2. Economic institutions such as the law of consecration and stewardship, tithing, cooperatives, the united order, and the welfare plan, have been provided to expedite the achievement of these goals. These institutions have one basic characteristic in common: they are cooperative, communal, or communitarian, rather than capitalistic.

3. The success of the institutions is conditional upon the success of members in changing their attitudes and behavior. Members must first develop brotherly love and put aside selfishness and laziness. The institutions will then provide a framework in which the desired goals may be achieved.

4. Tithing and the welfare plan are lesser institutions reflecting the level of preparation of Church members. Members must prepare themselves to someday live the "more perfect" law of consecration and stewardship.

The Constitution

The Mormon belief in the inspired nature of the Constitution of the United States is well documented.[22] In order to develop our model, however, it is necessary to identify the purposes for which the Constitution has been established. The basic scriptural statement is that the Constitution was "established, and should be maintained for the rights and protection of all flesh, according to just and holy principles" (D&C 101:77). The rights referred to are elaborated in the Doctrine and Covenants section 134, "A Declaration of Beliefs regarding Governments and Laws." The most concise statement lists the rights as "the free exercise of conscience, the right and control of property, and the protection of life" (D&C 134:2). Other scriptural statements stress free agency, personal freedom, and freedom of religion (D&C 101:78, 79–80; 134:4). These individual rights are guaranteed in the Constitution by the Bill of Rights, particularly Amendments 1, 4, and 5, and by the Thirteenth and Fourteenth Amendments.

The Constitution is important to Mormons because it guarantees them the right to live the laws of God, laws which may allow or require both religious and economic institutions. Mormons believe that the kingdom of God will one day rule the earth. Until that day, the City of God must be built within a larger "host" society. To be compatible with the City of God, the host must have one essential characteristic: it must guarantee the right to withdraw from it. By *withdrawal* I do not mean physical removal or political secession, but attitudinal, behavioral, and institutional withdrawal from the secular society, allowing, in the words of the eleventh Article of Faith, "all men the same privilege, let them worship how, where, or what they may." The system established by the Constitution helps to ensure that society will meet this essential condition.

Given Mormon beliefs about the Constitution, the ideal society, and the relationship of individuals to institutions, it is possible to predict Mormon policy and attitudes toward both the internal system and the external or host society. The basic assumptions are as follows:

1. Men and women should strive to attain the goals of the ideal Christian community: brotherly love, elimination of poverty, economic equality, and group economic self-sufficiency.

2. God, through the Church, will provide economic institutions to assist in attaining these goals.

3. To make these institutions work, individuals must put aside feelings of selfishness, laziness, envy, and greed.

4. The institutions must be established in the context of a host society—a larger legal, economic, and social system.

5. The Constitution provides a legal system which allows people to withdraw institutionally and attitudinally from the host society.

Under these assumptions, Mormons will strive to maintain and defend constitutional laws, in particular those laws which protect their rights to withdraw from the attitudes and institutions of society and to support and maintain a host economic system compatible with building the City of God. While supporting the maintenance of compatible host legal and economic systems, Mormons will withdraw from the host society through—

1. developing industry, selflessness, and brotherly love, while resisting attitudes of selfishness, greed, envy, and sloth prevailing in the host society;

2. establishing institutions designed to assist men and women in achieving the goals of the ideal society: economic equality, group self-sufficiency, and elimination of poverty.

This predicted pattern of behavior can now be tested by looking at Mormon economic history.

The Mormon Experience

When the doctrine of states' rights denied the Mormons protection and redress in Missouri and Illinois, Joseph Smith rejected that doctrine, maintaining that the federal government had both the power and the duty to guarantee the constitutional rights of all American citizens—even Mormons.[23] When the Mormons were driven from the United States, they went west, not to escape the Constitution, but to return to it. In an 1846 letter to Colonel Thomas L. Kane, Brigham Young stated:

> We love the constitution of our country, but are opposed to mobocracy; and will not live under such oppression as we have done. We are willing to have the banner of the U.S. Constitution float over us. If the government of the U.S. is disposed to do us good; we can do them as much good as they can us.[24]

That same summer President Young wrote to President James K. Polk, stating the Mormons' intention to apply for territorial status as soon as they were settled in the Great Basin.[25] In 1849 a constitutional convention approved the Constitution of the State of Deseret.[26] Later that year a memorial was sent to Congress seeking statehood rather than territorial status, probably because the same doctrine of states' rights which had earlier denied Mormons their constitutional privileges could now be used to guarantee them.[27] Territorial status instead of statehood was the result of the first petition; but the Mormons persisted, and constitutional conventions were held in 1856, 1862, 1872, 1882, 1887, and 1895. During that period Utah petitioned Congress for statehood at least ten times.[28] A reading of the constitutions from the various conventions shows the intent to guarantee the rights denied to the Mormons in the Midwest.[29]

The imposition of a territorial government rather than statehood was viewed by Mormons as an infringement on their constitutional right to home rule, particularly when gentile officials were appointed to govern them. Mormons viewed these officials as immoral, incompetent, vengeful Mormon-haters, and protested bitterly.[30] On the other hand, Mormons continued to elect and sustain their own "ghost government" of the State of Deseret and were considered by many to be in open rebellion against the government of the United States and in violation of its laws.[31] Through it all, Mormons invariably maintained their allegiance to the United States. They denied breaking any law.[32]

The Morrill Law of 1862, the Edmunds Law of 1882, and the Edmunds-Tucker Law of 1887 forced upon Mormons the choice of breaking the law of the land or breaking the law of God. They chose to break the law of the land, believing that God would not require them to obey a law which abrogated their rights to freedom of religion under the First Amendment (see D&C 58:21; 98:5-7; Articles of Faith, 12). Mormons therefore were stunned when the Supreme Court upheld the constitutionality of the Morrill Law in an 1879 test case, *Reynolds* v. *United States*. To the Mormons, the application of antipolygamy laws violated more than freedom of religion. They were *ex post facto* laws, assuming persons guilty until proved innocent, imposing excessive bail, making a mockery of trial by jury, requiring a wife to testify against her husband, imposing religious test oaths, depriving individuals of property and liberty without due process, and finally, attempting to disenfranchise the membership of the Church.[33] Mormons thus continued to violate these laws, steadfastly maintaining their constitutional right to establish an institution which, though it might offend individuals, would not injure those individuals or their society.[34]

The Manifesto of 1890 ended the polygamy issue. Statehood soon followed, and Mormons were finally guaranteed their full constitutional rights. Twentieth-century Mormons have not experienced such a direct attack upon their institutions and constitutional rights. They have been concerned about constitutional rights in general, however, focusing at various times on the outside threat of totalitarianism and on the inside threat of government power.

Two recent issues illustrate these concerns. The first has to do with the constitutionality of the federal income tax. In recent years some members of the Mormon Church have apparently refused to pay their income taxes, presumably on the grounds that the tax is directly unconstitutional or that it violates constitutional rights.[35] Church authorities recently issued a policy statement reminding members that the federal income tax laws had consistently been upheld as constitutional, and urging all members to comply. Failure to comply with the tax laws could be cause for Church disciplinary action.[36]

The second concern seems more serious. On 16 October 1975, officials of Brigham Young University announced that the University would not comply with certain regulations issued under Title IX of the Education Amendments Act of 1972 by the United States Department of Health, Education, and Welfare. Title IX deals with sex discrimination in education. The refusal to comply was based on three contentions:

1. Some of the regulations are unlawful because they exceed the department's statutory authority under Title IX.

2. Some of the regulations are unconstitutional because they violate the due process clause or the constitutional guarantee of religious freedom.

3. Some of the regulations prohibit or interfere with the teaching or practice of high moral principles, such as honesty, integrity, and chastity.[37]

After endorsing the goal of equal opportunity for both men and women in education and employment, and listing the positive steps taken to implement the goal, the published notification states the objections to the regulations in general and declares:

> Nevertheless, we voluntarily choose to follow many of the regulations because we believe them to embody policies which are fair and just. But where we believe the regulations are unconstitutional or illegal and where they prohibit or interfere with the teaching or practice of high moral principles, we will not follow them.[38]

The notification concludes with a defense of the legality of BYU's stand, and a restatement of the position of the Church on obedience to law:

> Our church teaches the necessity of "obeying, honoring, and sustaining the law" (Articles of Faith 12) and of "befriending that law which is the constitutional law of the land" (Doc. & Cov. 98:6). Therefore, we will comply with any regulation ultimately sustained as lawful by the courts of the United States. In the interim we will follow the policies outlined above, which represent our best judgment on the meaning of the constitution and laws that govern us.[39]

There are several points to be made here. First, the document seems to place regulations or laws into three categories, two stated and one implied.

The stated categories are:

1. Laws or regulations that are clearly constitutional or, though possibly unlawful, embody policies or principles which are fair and just.

2. Those which are believed to be unconstitutional or illegal and which violate such essential rights as freedom of religion, due process, and the teaching or practice of high moral principles.

The third, implied category apparently contains:

3. "Meddlesome" laws or regulations which are believed to be unconstitutional or illegal, but which do not violate essential rights.

The distinction between the second and third categories centers on the definition of "essential rights." In this particular case, the regulations which come under the second category are those which violate the essential right of a religious body to establish a private educational institution to foster the teaching and practice of high moral principles.[40] The University's refusal to comply with regulations in category two places this example squarely within the predicted pattern—that Mormons will strive to maintain and defend constitutional laws, in particular those laws which protect the (essential) rights of individuals to withdraw from the attitudes and institutions of society.

A second point is the stated intention of the University to comply with any regulation ultimately sustained as lawful by the courts of the United States.

The University stated its voluntary compliance with regulations in category one, refused to comply with those in category two, and by implication agreed to comply with regulations falling into the third category, presumably not deeming it vital to test their legality or constitutionality through direct noncompliance.[41] Any regulation eventually sustained by the courts as lawful and constitutional, however, would be observed, as required by Church doctrine.

Recall the previous two examples. The refusal of the Church to support the stand of violators of the income tax laws can be explained in two ways. First, the laws have been upheld by the courts as constitutional; second, if there were still a question about the constitutionality of the laws, they would fall into the third category and should be obeyed anyway.

In the polygamy example, the above categorizations do not hold. The antipolygamy laws were upheld as constitutional; yet Mormons continued to violate them. The model of behavior thus fails to predict whether Mormons, in defense of their constitutional rights, will break the law of the land.

The key problem here is the interpretation of "constitutionality." Mormons believe in obeying the law of the land which is constitutional; but constitutional by whose definition? The answer is inherent in the necessity of existing within a larger society (assumption four): the society at large, or more specifically, the courts will determine the constitutionality of the law. Consistency of this conclusion with the original results requires one more assumption—that the laws of the land will not conflict with the laws of God. The relevant scripture states: "Let no man break the laws of the land, for he that keepeth the laws of God hath no need to break the laws of the land" (D&C 58:21). The addition of this assumption to the model leads to an additional behavioral result: that Mormons will not knowingly violate a law upheld by the courts as constitutional.

Church policy has been consistent with this predicted behavior in all examples except that of polygamy. In that case, the failure of the model to predict behavior correctly was clearly a direct consequence of the failure of the last assumption. After the 1879 test case, the world no longer conformed to Mormon assumptions. But the Mormons, clinging stubbornly to their world view, refused to accept the ruling of the courts and continued to violate the laws which, in their view, must have been unconstitutional because they interfered with the law of God. The failure of one assumption threatened others. Neither side would give in, and the situation became intolerable, undermining the continued existence in society of all Mormon institutions. The Manifesto was necessary, and when it came it did not imply new assumptions, but rather restored the validity of the old.

The initial assumptions led to the prediction that Mormons will "support and maintain a host economic system compatible with building the City of God"—that is, a system which will allow the formation of alternative economic institutions. There are two necessary conditions for a compatible host system. First, the host economy must be basically unplanned. Here I am referring to central planning, since planning per se exists in any economy at some level of disaggregation. Second, the rights of private use and disposition of property must exist; otherwise, economic property cannot be transferred to nor retained in nonconforming uses.

What economic systems meet the foregoing conditions? Capitalism clearly qualifies; it is basically unplanned, relying on voluntary market transactions to determine prices and allocate resources. The private property ownership inherent in capitalism meets the second criterion. Socialism of the Soviet type clearly fails to meet the conditions. The success of a centrally planned economy is dependent upon adherence to the plan. Interdependencies in a modern economy and the inflexibility of central planning makes nonconformance extremely costly.[42] The automatic market mechanism can easily adjust to institutional withdrawal; the inflexible central plan cannot. Thus we observe state, rather than private, control over the use and disposition of property. A system of decentralized, largely independent production regions, such as exist in China, may meet the first criterion, but not the second.[43]

Another possibility may be a system of producer cooperatives, where the individual cooperatives and consumers interact through markets. Such a system must meet the second condition, also—the rights of private use and disposition of property. This would seem to rule out the Yugoslav model.[44] A system of producer cooperatives which met both criteria would necessarily be voluntary—not very different, for these purposes, from capitalism.[45]

In general, the various brands of mixed economies—democratic socialism, planned capitalism, corporatism, and market socialism—are unsuited as host economies to the extent that they employ direct planning and control, and to the degree that they interfere with private rights to use and dispose of property. Ironically, the control over the disposition of property and the degree of planning characteristic of Mormon economic institutions violate the essential criteria for a host economy.[46]

In assessing the consistency of Mormon policy and behavior with the predictions of the model, statements or policies which relate directly to the maintenance of a compatible host economic system should be distinguished from statements which evaluate attitudes or other characteristics of the existing host economy.

The first point in this assessment is that Mormon support of the Constitution is also support of a compatible host economic system. The private property rights guaranteed by the Fifth and Fourteenth Amendments meet the second necessary condition. The first condition is met by the limitation of economic regulation implied in the Bill of Rights, by the Fourteenth Amendment, and by a federal system with specific powers enumerated, limited, and diffused between state and federal governments and among various branches thereof.[47]

In the nineteenth century there were few, if any, statements reflecting Mormon attitudes toward compatible host systems, except in the context of the constitutional rights and powers just mentioned. In the twentieth century, however, there is a growing concern over the increased power and size of the federal government, particularly as embodied in regulatory agencies. The HEW incident is but one example of that sentiment.[48] Of even greater concern has been the threat of communism. Church leaders have continually pointed out the absence, in that system, of personal rights such as the ownership and control of private property and freedom of religion. At the same time, there has been a tendency to extol the benefits of capitalism—private property, high productivity, and a market system.[49] These expressions are all clearly consistent with predicted behavior.

One prediction implied by the initial assumptions was that:

> While supporting the maintenance of compatible host legal and economic systems, Mormons will withdraw from the host society through—
> 1. developing industry, selflessness, and brotherly love, while resisting attitudes of selfishness, greed, envy, and sloth prevailing in the host society;
> 2. establishing institutions designed to assist men and women in achieving the goals of the ideal society: economic equality, group self-sufficiency, and the elimination of poverty.

Mormon economic institutions were reviewed in the first part of this essay. In the last century the law of consecration and stewardship, mercantile and manufacturing cooperatives, the united order, and Zion's Central Board of Trade were the important economic institutions. The law of tithing and an expanding Church welfare plan serve the role in this century. The noneconomic institutions, including the Church Educational System, priesthood quorums, various auxiliary programs, home teaching, family home evening, and many other boards and committees, also fall under category two.

Turning to part one, I suggest that the principles of selflessness, brotherly love, and industry are deeply ingrained in the doctrine and teachings of the Mormon faith and need not be detailed here. The second part of the statement, resistance to the attitudes of the host society, is not as evident in Mormon history.

The nineteenth-century Mormon position on capitalism is generally characterized as antagonistic and defensive. While containing more than a grain of truth, this characterization is usually misinterpreted. The vital characteristics of capitalism as a host system—the rights of private use and disposition of property and the absence of government control or planning—were consistently defended by Mormons as part of the inspired Constitution. Brigham Young did not call for the elimination of the market system or the nationalization of all private property. To do so would have been institutionally suicidal. In supporting the maintenance of the basic characteristics of capitalism, Mormons were simply maintaining the possibility of withdrawing from the system through the establishment of their own noncapitalistic institutions.

The withdrawal from a host society requires attitudinal as well as institutional withdrawal. Thus, Brigham Young and other Church leaders attacked the attitudes of selfishness and greed characteristic of capitalism, but at the same time depended upon the basic institutional characteristics of capitalism for the very existence of their own noncapitalistic institutions. This is not as paradoxical as it may seem and is entirely consistent with predicted behavior.

In addition to attacking the attitudes of capitalism, Mormons often criticized the operating characteristics of the system. Price fluctuations, "ruinous competition," business cycles, strikes, unemployment, monopoly exploitation, poverty, income inequality, and concentration of wealth were all ascribed to capitalism and then condemned. Such attacks were nearly always made in conjunction with a comparison between capitalism and the ideal economic system.

These criticisms were not limited to the nineteenth century. During the 1930s a typical statement on the subject might blame the world's problems on the concentration of wealth inherent in capitalism and suggest that the problems could be overcome only by the reestablishment of the united order. Alternative economic systems such as socialism were never suggested as solutions to the problems, nor was increased government control over the economy.[50] In fact, increased government control has often been blamed for the ills of the system, especially in recent years. Intended to emphasize the differences between the institutions of the world and the ideal society, such attacks fall within the predictions of the model.

The differences observed in Mormon attitudes toward capitalism between the nineteenth and twentieth centuries are primarily differences in emphasis in response to changing conditions, rather than differences in substance. In the nineteenth century, the main concern was in achieving an attitudinal withdrawal to match the institutional withdrawal which had taken place. The ability to establish new institutions was evident, and the host economic system did not appear to be threatened by either outside ideological foe or inside government regulation. The emphasis, then, was on the shortcomings of capitalism relative to the ideal system, rather than on the strengths of capitalism as a host system.

In the twentieth century the situation is quite different. The economic institutions, tithing and the welfare program, are well established and well supported. They are, however, admittedly inferior to the law of consecration and stewardship, which Mormons believe will some day be re-established. Noneconomic institutions, mentioned earlier, are used effectively to foster attitudes essential in a Christian community. A primary concern is the threat, both external and internal, to the important characteristics of the host economy—characteristics which must be maintained if nonconforming institutions are to exist. Thus there is an emphasis on the basic strengths of capitalism as a host system relative to socialism or other alternatives, rather than on a comparison of capitalism to the ideal system.

Though consistent with the model, this emphasis has led to attitudes among some Mormons which are contrary to predicted behavior. Having been taught the superiority of capitalism as a host system, they begin to attribute capitalistic institutions, as well as the attitudes and operational characteristics of capitalism, to the ideal system. In my opinion, this confusion between the *host system* and the *ideal system* is serious.

I now ask the key question in this essay. Has there been a change in the Mormon world view from the last century to this? Do Mormons have a model of the relationship between man, God, and institutions which is different today than it was a hundred years ago? I think not. The model presented here, though admittedly incomplete, is consistent with observed Mormon attitudes and policies in both this century and the last. The predictions failed only once, in suggesting that Mormons would comply with the antipolygamy laws after the test case of 1879. It was argued that this failure was the result of the failure of one assumption, and that the Manifesto of 1890, far from representing a new world view, restored the validity of the old.

Let me conclude with some reactions to this analysis as an economist. One assumption on which economic theory can shed light states that the failure of institutions to fulfill their purposes can be attributed to the failure of individuals to change their attitudes and behavior—in effect, to become unselfish.

It can be demonstrated that utopian economic systems are likely to be faced with serious problems if the actors in the system make decisions based solely on their economic self-interest. The categories of likely problems include incentives, resource allocation, and capital accumulation—in general, economic efficiency.[51] Many of these problems are serious enough to make me doubt that such systems could operate at all, particularly in the context of an efficient host system like capitalism. Presumably, the problem of direct competition with the host economy could be reduced by attaining self-sufficiency.[52] But self-sufficiency has a double cost: the forfeiture of the gains from exchange, and the gains from specialization available through trade with the host economy.

It can also be demonstrated that most, and perhaps all, of the problems of efficiency in utopian systems disappear or are greatly minimized if individuals are not selfish.[53] The particular utopian system doesn't much matter. If men and women are unselfish, practically any system will work. At a very basic level, then, the assumption is correct: people fail, not institutions. In my opinion, discussions about the exact nature of the ideal economic system are basically sterile. If there has been a change in man's nature, any system will work; if individuals have not changed, none will.[54]

Finally, what are the implications of the model for economic policy? Since the important aspects of a host economic system are the rights of property and the absence of direct central planning, standard monetary and fiscal policies are acceptable. Direct intervention in the economy, if it results in a loss of flexibility or interferes with the right of private use or disposition of property, is unacceptable.[55] These are policy rules which tend to promote economic efficiency, and as an economist I am generally comfortable with them. There are two points, however, which should be raised. First, monopoly power in the economy may lead to a conflict between the goals of noninterference with property rights and the maintenance of flexibility in the system. Antitrust action which is intended to restore competitive characteristics to markets necessarily interferes with the rights of private use and disposition of property. This trade-off between the two primary characteristics of the host economy should be recognized.

Also important is the classic trade-off between equity and efficiency which accompanies income redistribution. Although equity is not an essential characteristic of a host economy, humanitarian concerns have led Church leaders to decry the existence of poverty and gross inequality in the society.[56] The foregoing analysis suggests that attempts to alleviate these conditions through redistribution of income be evaluated according to their impact on the maintenance of a compatible host economy. I should point out here that in the history of our country, improvement in the quality and availability of education, rather than direct income redistribution, provides the best explanation for the overall reduction of economic inequality. Within any employment group, however, the degree of unemployment experienced is the single most important cause of inequality.[57] Thus, economic policies which promote full employment without direct controls can reduce inequities in the host economy without interfering with flexibility or property rights.

The foregoing analysis leads me to four conclusions. First, of all economic systems, capitalism best meets the essential criteria of a host economy—lack of central planning and private property rights. Second, the Constitution helps guarantee that these conditions will continue to be met. Third, capitalism is not the ideal system. The institutions, attitudes, and operating characteristics of the ideal system are different from (and in many cases diametrically opposed to) those of capitalism. Fourth, there was not a change from the nineteenth to the twentieth centuries in the way Mormons view the relationship between God, individuals, and institutions.

---

1. Leonard J. Arrington, "Early Mormon Communitarianism: The Law of Consecration and Stewardship," *Western Humanities Review*, 5 (April 1953):342. For an excellent comprehensive work on the history of economic cooperation in Mormon history, see Leonard J. Arrington, Feramorz Y. Fox, and Dean May, *Building the City of God: Community and Cooperation among the Mormons* (Salt Lake City: Deseret Book, 1976).

2. D&C 42; see also Arrington, "Early Mormon Communitarianism," pp. 342–43.

3. Arrington, "Early Mormon Communitarianism," pp. 343–44.

4. Ibid., pp. 346, 351–55. It is difficult to identify exactly what kind of ownership is implied. The property right was apparently not usufruct, since restrictions were placed on the income from the property: the surplus had to be consecrated. The stewardship document was called a "lease and loan," with real property "leased" and personal property "loaned" to the steward. If the steward transgressed, he forfeited all claim to the real property and agreed to pay to the Church the value of the personal property. There were also restrictions on inheritance, and transfers were not allowed. Jonathan Hughes ("Comments" delivered at Conference on Economics and the Mormon Culture, October 6, 1975, Brigham Young University) finds a later (1856) consecration deed to be an example of subinfeudation, not legal in the United States ever, except in Maryland, Delaware, and Pennsylvania in colonial times. Here the ultimate "donor" was expected to be the federal government. The Church barred automatic inheritance of heirs, making title to the land escheat to itself.

5. Arrington, "Early Mormon Communitarianism," pp. 349–55. The Church had legal difficulty with the "lease and loan" documents, and some apostates sued successfully in the courts for the return of their entire consecration. In response to this problem, in 1833 a "warranty deed in fee simple" replaced the "lease and loan" document. See also Arrington et al., *Building the City of God*, ch. 2.

6. Arrington, "Early Mormon Communitarianism," pp. 359–61. Brigham Young stated: "I was present at the time the revelation came for the brethren to give their surplus property into the hands of the Bishops for the building up of Zion, but I never knew a man yet who had a dollar of surplus property. No matter how much one might have he wanted all he had for himself, for his children, his grand-children, and so forth" (*Journal of Discourses*, 26 vols. [London: Latter-day Saints' Book Depot, 1855–86], 16:11).

7. Arrington, "Early Mormon Communitarianism," p. 363. A member was to donate the equivalent of one-tenth of his possessions when he was converted, and one-tenth of his annual increase (or more) thereafter.

8. Ibid., pp. 363–68. Arrington suggests that the law of consecration and stewardship was not economically feasible in Nauvoo because of the state of Church resources, financial and otherwise.

9. Arrington et al., *Building the City of God*, pp. 66, 75. Arrington estimates that about 2,700 of 7,000 heads of families filed consecration deeds.

10. Ibid., ch. 4. Until 1869, when land laws of the United States were made applicable to the Utah Territory, lands were held only by squatter's rights.

11. Ibid., ch. 5.

12. Ibid., appendix IV.

13. L. Dwight Israelsen, "Economics of the United Order," Working Paper, Department of Economics, Brigham Young University, October 1975, appendix 4. See also L. Dwight Israelsen, "An Economic Analysis of the United Order," *Brigham Young University Studies*, 18, no. 4 (Summer 1978), pp. 536–61.

14. L. Dwight Israelsen, "Collectives, Communes, and Incentives," *Journal of Comparative Economics*, forthcoming.

15. Arrington et al., *Building the City of God*, ch. 12. Other communal orders were established at Price City, Springdale, Kingston, Kanab, Monroe, Richfield, and Joseph, Utah; Bunkerville, Nevada; and Joseph City, Sunset, Brigham City, Obed, Woodruff, Snowflake, and Taylor, Arizona (Israelsen, "Economic Analysis of the United Order," n. 14).

16. L. Dwight Israelsen, "The Problem of Underinvestment in the Mormon United Order," abstract in *Proceedings of the Utah Academy of Sciences, Arts, and Letters* 53, part 2 (Fall 1976).

17. Israelsen, "Economics of the United Order," p. 11, nn. 15–17.

18. Ibid., p. 13. Most united orders failed within a year or two. The longest-lived branch of the order was in Logan, Utah, a joint enterprise of the Second and Third Wards which was established in 1875 and sold out to private interests in 1909 (Ibid., p. 5).

19. Ibid., p. 13, nn. 20, 1.

20. It can be demonstrated that producer cooperatives and other utopian economic systems will be plagued with various types of inefficiencies if the members are selfish. If they are unselfish, the problems disappear (see Israelsen, "Collectives, Communes, and Incentives").

21. Leonard J. Arrington, *Great Basin Kingdom* (Cambridge, Mass.: Harvard University Press, 1958), pp. 341–49.

22. See, for example, Noel B. Reynolds, "The Doctrine of an Inspired Constitution," *Brigham Young University Studies* (Spring 1976).

23. See, for example, Joseph Smith to John C. Calhoun, 2 January 1844, in *History of The Church of Jesus Christ of Latter-day Saints*, ed. B. H. Roberts, 7 vols. (Salt Lake City: The Church of Jesus Christ of Latter-day Saints, 1932–51), 6:159–60.

24. *LDS Journal History*, 7 August 1846, Church Archives, The Church of Jesus Christ of Latter-day Saints, Salt Lake City, Utah.

25. Gustive O. Larson, *The Americanization of Utah for Statehood* (San Marino, Calif.: Huntington Library, 1971), p. 2.

26. *LDS Journal History*, 8 March 1849.

27. Larson, *Americanization of Utah*, p. 6.

28. Ibid., pp. 59, 60, 91, 97, 217–22, 294–96.

29. *LDS Journal History*, 8 March 1949, 30 June 1846; "Constitution of the State of Deseret," 1862, 1872, Church Archives; "Constitution of the State of Utah," 1882, 1887, Church Archives.

30. For example, Judge W. W. Drummond was referred to as an "infamous scoundrel and dastardly wretch," a "beastly criminal," "horrible monster," "black-hearted judge," "poor wretch," "lying, adulterous, murderous fiend," "loathsome specimen of humanity," etc. (Norman F. Furniss, *The Mormon Conflict* [New Haven, Conn.: Yale University Press, 1960], p. 54). See also *LDS Journal History*, 18 February 1854; discourse by Heber C. Kimball, *Journal of Discourses*, 5:158–65; etc.

31. The "ghost government" continued until 1870 (Larson, *Americanization of Utah*, pp. 29, 31).

32. See, for example, ibid., pp. 61–89.

33. The test oath was declared "null and void" by the Supreme Court in 1885, in *Jesse J. Murphy* v. *Alexander Ramsey et al.* Another interesting application of antipolygamy laws was the principle of segregation, that is, dividing the time period during which the offense took place into subperiods, with a separate charge for each subperiod. This policy was found unconstitutional by the Supreme Court in 1887.

34. Nearly any speech of the period by a Church leader or accused polygamist will serve as a reference. For example, Rudger Clawson, when asked if there was any reason why judgment should not be pronounced, stated: "I very much regret that the laws of my country should come in conflict with the laws of God; but whenever they do, I shall invariably choose the latter. If I did not so express myself, I should feel unworthy of the cause I represent. . . . The law of 1862 and the Edmunds Law were expressly designed to operate against marriage as practiced and believed by the Latter-day Saints. They are therefore, unconstitutional, and, of course, cannot command the respect that a Constitutional law would" (Larson, *Americanization of Utah*, p. 109).

35. The federal income tax is provided for by the Sixteenth Amendment.

36. Letter from the First Presidency of The Church of Jesus Christ of Latter-day Saints to all stake and mission presidents in the United States, 19 September 1975.

37. "Notification of Brigham Young University Policy of Non-Discrimination on the Basis of Sex," published in various newspapers, 18, 19 October 1975.

38. Ibid.

39. Ibid.

40. Ibid.

41. Ibid.

42. The failure of any unit in the economy to conform to the plan will lead to the inability of a large number of other units to conform to the plan.

43. We really don't know the extent of planning in the Chinese economy. It is clearly less centralized than the Soviet Union, and more centralized than the United States, but the planning apparently takes place mainly at the regional level.

44. There are few limits on the use of property by a cooperative. The disposition of property, or use of property privately, is severely restricted.

45. There is nothing about a capitalist economy which would prevent the organization of voluntary producer cooperatives. In fact, groups in our economy form voluntary producer cooperatives quite regularly.

46. For a good picture of the degree of planning and control in the Mormon economic institutions, see Arrington, *Great Basin Kingdom*.

47. In recent years, the commerce clause has been interpreted quite broadly and has given considerable power to regulatory agencies.

48. A related example is the concern expressed by Church leaders over federal aid to education and the various regulations the acceptance of such aid entails. For that reason the Church Educational System does not accept direct government grants.

49. The productivity aspects aren't as important in the context of this model as are the other two. Brigham Young seemed to feel that the productivity of capitalism in his day was not especially high.

50. One attack on the ills of capitalism was tempered by warnings that just because there were problems in the economy, members of the Church should not become "bolsheviks" (Melvin J. Ballard, conference address, June 19, 1932). We have at least one example, however, where the united order was referred to as "the higher socialism" (see article by John A. Widtsoe, *Deseret News*, 18 March 1933).

51. Israelsen, "Economics of the United Order," pp. 6–8, appendices 1–3. See also Israelsen, "Collectives, Communes, and Incentives."

52. Self-sufficiency was a goal of the Mormon economic experiments (see Arrington, "Early Mormon Communitarianism," p. 342; Arrington et al., *Building the City of God*, chs. 5, 7, 15; Israelsen, "Economics of the United Order," pp. 10, 11, appendix 6).

53. See, for example, Israelsen, "Economics of of the United Order," p. 24, n. 40. This seems to explain the success of the Orderville united order. Karl Marx believed that the elimination of both selfishness and scarcity would be necessary in the transition from socialism to communism. This seems rather redundant, since only a perverse person would exhibit selfish behavior in the absence of scarcity.

54. This is not to say that the subject is not inherently interesting. The point is that although an economist may be well qualified to provide economic explanations for the failure of utopian systems, he is not particularly well qualified to discuss the merits of alternative utopian organizations when the actors in the system are not selfish. (Even here I must qualify the statement. If there are sources of economic inefficiency which have nothing to do with incentives and selfish behavior, they will not necessarily disappear with the disappearance of selfishness. For example, if property is reallocated from skilled, high-productivity individuals to low-productivity, unskilled individuals, total output will fall. The loss of economic welfare which results from self-sufficiency also falls into this category, having nothing to do with self-ishness.)

55. Standard macroeconomic fiscal and monetary policies help control fluctuations in the economy by working through markets. Direct controls, on the other hand, generally interfere with the smooth operation of markets, leading to distortions which are themselves sometimes used as reasons for further controls. An example of this type of control is the phases of price controls which we endured under the Nixon administration. The controls exacerbated inflationary pressures in some markets, and the existence of those increased pressures was cited as a reason for not removing the controls.

56. Poverty and gross inequality can also lead to dissatisfaction among the disadvantaged, which may threaten the stability and even the continued existence of a socioeconomic system.

57. Paul A. Samuelson, *Economics*, 8th ed. (New York: McGraw-Hill Book Co., 1970), pp. 769, 771.

The Constitution
as Change

William Clayton Kimball, *a political scientist, does not have a mechanistic view of the Constitution. He has what he calls an organic and behavioral view. In his essay he explores the relationship of our constitutional document to our American constitutional culture. He explains and discusses the basic nature of the Constitution and how it relates to change. Political change, he says, is largely a by-product of social change and not the reverse. To understand the dynamics of political change, he says, one must look at demographic shifts, technological innovation, economic patterns, and so forth. Public compliance and legitimacy are two main problems in constitutional change, says Kimball. He supports these assertions with historical examples and then focuses specifically on the Equal Rights Amendment.*

Professor Kimball is a professor in the Department of Government at Bentley College in Waltham, Massachusetts. He has his Ph.D. from Harvard University and teaches American and constitutional law at Bentley College.

MOST AMERICANS THINK of constitutions as specific documents which can be hung on walls or included as an appendix in textbooks. We feel comfortable saying such things as "In the Constitution it says . . ." and "Do you have a copy of the Constitution handy?" But there are other ways to think of constitutions. Aristotle, for example, thought of them in a very general sense. He used the word the way we do when we say that a person has a "strong constitution" or a "weak constitution." His constitutions (he collected as many examples as he could acquire) were neither formal organizational charts, nor even collections of laws. Rather, they were extensive summaries and histories of the various manifestations of political life in specific societies. If we were to describe "the American Constitution" as Aristotle described the constitution of Athens, we would have to range far beyond formal legal elements to include what we today call political culture and behavior.[1]

Thus, Aristotle would not be able to gather together the materials on a city-state in Greece just once. If he wanted to keep his work current he would have to revise it periodically to take account of the changes that had occurred. The typical American view is that the Constitution was written in 1787 and has been changed only twenty-six times since then. It would make no sense to us to include such things as census data, technological innovations, or a treatment of grants-in-aid in a description of our constitution. This, as we shall see, is one reason why political change is so difficult for us to explain in constitutional terms.

This paper will explore the relationship between our American Constitution and political change. The purpose of the exploration is to examine the nature of political change and the problems it poses for our system.

I

The U.S. Constitution, when it went into effect in the late eighteenth century, was itself an experiment in political change. Dissatisfaction with the weak national governmental structure and the resulting economic and political instability impelled the experiment. But the new document and the governmental structure it mandated did not emerge into a vacuum. They were superimposed on an active political culture and were grounded on an acute understanding of the political behavior and beliefs of the American people of that time. The words of the document quickly became the framework within which those beliefs and that behavior developed.

Before we proceed, a distinction must be made between the constitutional document (the usually understood meaning of *constitution*), "constitutional institutions" (those created by the document plus those not mentioned or foreseen, such as political parties and interest groups), and the "constitutional culture" (accepted behaviors, shared attitudes, private organizations, ideals, etc.). One might think of them as three concentric circles with the document at the center, embedded in a set of legitimate institutions, and both enveloped and permeated by the broader political culture.[2] Throughout our history the document has been changed very little. But the institutions and the culture have changed greatly.

One's very attitude toward change—how it takes place, and how its effects are manifested in the political system—depends, ultimately, on the model of reality one accepts.[3] Glendon Schubert suggests that there are basically three models of thinking about politics (and the Constitution) in the American tradition, each one tied to successive historical periods, and each employing distinctive metaphors to express it:[4]

1. The first model, which captivated the generation which framed the Constitution, uses the metaphors of classical physics.[5] If something is wrong, a bit of tinkering with the formal mechanisms of government (constitutions and laws) will set it right. This model (and its metaphors) continues to dominate most discussions about laws, constitutions, and change.

2. The second model is derived from the dominant nineteenth-century metaphor of the biological organism as the paradigm of reality. Change is gradual but inexorable. A change in one part of the social organism will produce changes throughout, perhaps unforeseen and unwanted. Intentional change is far more difficult to conceptualize using this model, while it is relatively clear-cut using the mechanical model of the eighteenth century.

3. The third model is the most recent, and the least specific. This model uses the language and imagery of cybernetics and communications theory,[6] and seeks to provide a more flexible view of political and social reality than the mechanical and organic models provide. One speaks here of feedback, of public policy norms, or aggregate "behaviors" and the like.[7]

The history of the United States is replete with vast changes. Political institutions and customs have come into existence within the framework of the original document with no formal alteration of that document. The first, or mechanistic, model cannot explain these changes. Political change (i.e., change which clearly affects governmental processes and institutions), while clearly an integral part of the overall process of change, far more often comes as the result of prior change in the constitutional culture. That is, by the time an observable change has taken place in the formal or structural elements of government, the causal changes have long since occurred, very often in areas we would call nonpolitical. Political change is a necessary but not a sufficient factor to explain why our political culture today is not what it was a score of years ago.

To understand the dynamics of change one must concentrate on such things as demographic shifts, technological innovations, economic dislocations (and locations), alterations in the moral fabric of society, and so on. Each causal element of change, while it may be studied in isolation, is never really isolated. The relationship between such elements is always synergistic. For example, the "baby boom" of the late 1940s and early 1950s, which produced such incredible strains on our educational, social, and political institutions in the late 1950s and 1960s, certainly would not have occurred without the dislocations of World War II, the technological impact of war-related inventions, a moral climate which was unconcerned with population expansion, and the economic improvement over the 1930s.[8]

We do not understand the complexities of change. We do realize that when change takes place it is caused by factors largely beyond the control and perhaps the comprehension of both the average man and the political leadership of a society. The most common reaction in the face of change is to personalize it: "It's all Roosevelt's fault" or "Why didn't Eisenhower do something about it?" The common attitude toward political change is anthropocentric: we see change most clearly in terms of the succession of presidents, the appointment of new justices to the Supreme Court, and electoral contests which are easily personalized. Such a view is not completely inaccurate, of course; but who can doubt that the seminal causes of change in our system transcend any man, any group, or any number of governmental policies? Yet, in turn, any man (a Lee Harvey Oswald), any group (the NAACP), or any governmental policy (Medicare) becomes another factor in the synergistic matrix which brings about change. One cannot isolate political change. History, economics, sociology, psychology—many disciplines must be integrated to deal with the real complexity inherent in the problem of explaining change.[9]

II

It has become a truism to comment on the flexibility of the United States Constitution. The Constitution is as much a symbol as it is a charter of government. We have followed a sort of collective agreement through-out our history to leave the basic document (which includes the first ten amendments, the Bill of Rights) relatively unencumbered by textual changes. At the same time, we have been highly creative in altering in-stitutions and in adding to the methods of governing. The framers of the Constitution did not seek to bind posterity.[10] Even though we still go through the motions in our constitutional law of trying to ascertain the in-tentions of the framers, few of their ideas speak to our problems today. But this is not a cynical attitude. Far more is involved in the search for "con-stitutionality" than a mechanical comparison of current innovations with traditional methods and ideals. It adds a very special element to the United States system which is crucial to our success.

> Political continuity and the stability and predictability that accompany it are themselves peculiar virtues of American political life, and they must always be weighed in the balance when deciding whether new so-lutions are really worthwhile. . . . Constitutional debate thus also serves as a warning that in judging the desirability of a statute, we must consid-er not only how it operates today but how it will affect our long-range goals and permanent values. . . . Our written constitution and its contin-ued political impact are important guarantees that our preoccupation with the pressing problems of the moment will not lead to solutions that ignore the basic questions of where we have been and where we want to go.[11]

Neither the president, the Congress, nor the Supreme Court (nor any of the institutions not described in the original document) can make policy suc-cessfully if their actions do not meet with the approval and acceptance of the people of the United States, at least over the long run. The Constitution as a political reality—the combination of document, institutions, and cul-ture—actually rests on the tolerance and will and intentions of the people of the country, that is, on those who are present, voting, and obeying or dis-obeying. While the Constitution usually limits the agents of the people, it limits the people of the United States in their sovereign capacity only as long as they accept those limits. The Constitution remains an instrument of the people, just as it was in 1789. As long as they cherish the principles of the Constitution, it will be the symbol of self-government and freedom. As long as they believe in the importance of the Constitution, it will continue to limit government.

We might look at some cogent examples of this point. The loss of power which President Nixon suffered, which came long before he left office, demonstrates the importance of public support as the cornerstone of presidential power. Nixon had every formal and informal power in July of 1974 that he had had in January of 1973, but the difference in his capacity to exercise that power was enormous. And before the details of the events prior to the Watergate break-in, as well as the excesses of the cover-up, began to permeate the public's awareness, Congress was equally unable to challenge the president's position because it did not have public support.[12] The Supreme Court, that "least dangerous branch," as Hamilton called it, is theoretically the least dependent of the three branches on public or popular support. But the Court has never strayed far from the general consensus in the country since it began handing down decisions.[13]

The power of democratic government rests on its legitimacy—on the acceptance of its actions by the people. What the Constitution does, in one sense, is to generate certain beliefs and expectations about the process by which governmental decisions ought to be made. When these procedures are duly followed, acceptance usually follows, unless violent passions are aroused. If, in fact, the decisions made are abhorrent to large numbers of people, all the proper procedure in the world will not generate compliance. Compliance, which is the usual evidence of legitimacy, is a crucial support of constitutionality.

As we have noted, vast changes have taken place in our institutions and in our political habits within the framework of the constitutional document without a word of the document having been altered. Yet these changes have been ratified by public acceptance. Federalism, for example, which was the most distinctive American contribution to the techniques of governing, has undergone constant change as the nation has grown and its economic life has changed. The federalism of Andrew Jackson's time was very different from the federalism a century later when Franklin Roosevelt was president. The people of the 1830s would never have accepted the federalism of the 1930s as legitimate. But the people of the 1930s could not have endured the 1830s federal structure. It cannot be said, therefore, that one was "constitutional" and the other was not. Each grew out of the conditions of American society at the time. Those today who feel that modern federalism does not deserve the name perhaps do not understand the decentralized impact of political parties, Congress, and the use of governmental contracts in our system.[14]

The argument being advanced would suggest, then, that changes—whether in the basic patterns of federalism, the relationships between presidents and Congress, or the shifting, extraconstitutional operations of political parties and interest groups—come in response to changes in the "constitutional culture" which is the environment of government. Changes which might grow out of technological advances and population shifts would first have impact on the culture, then on institutions, and finally, if there is not enough flexibility to accommodate the changes, on the central and most permanent part of the system, the document itself.

It was asserted above that compliance is a crucial element of legitimacy. Generally, they are seen as being quite similar. But, of course, legitimacy does not guarantee compliance. The sign which tells the driver that he is approaching a school zone may or may not entice him to lower his speed. He means no challenge to the legitimacy of that speed notice. Further, repeated reminders of the national speed limit are obviously legitimate, but are just as obviously ignored. Any governmental decision or policy stands or falls in terms of the effective compliance it elicits. Our history is full of examples of "orders" from courts, executives, and legislatures which were not obeyed because public (or group) support was lacking. Examples of this lack of compliance would include:

1. Massive noncompliance with the Supreme Court's decisions dealing with religious exercises in public schools. Today there are probably far more districts which prescribe prayers in public schools than there were in 1962 when the first case was decided.[15]

2. The saga of desegregation, both before and after the Supreme Court declared it unconstitutional, demonstrates the difficulty of enforcing orders on a population unwilling to comply. In states where segregation was the law, it took well over a decade before compliance was compelled. The country is now troubled by other forms of segregation, and the bitterness of local conflicts shows that the problem of compliance is a serious one.[16]

3. Mormon history contains perhaps the most interesting example of massive disobedience to governmental orders. Disobedience continued long after the Supreme Court decision in *Reynolds* v. *U.S.*,[17] and after the Church itself had renounced the practice of polygamy.

4. The number of young men who fled this country in the 1960s because of the combination of the draft laws and the war in Vietnam is large enough, regardless of one's personal attitude toward them, to stand as an example of massive noncompliance.

The point is simple. If the people of the United States, or the part thereof affected, will not obey a law, a court order, or even a constitutional provision, those governmental orders, legitimate as they may be, are not effective. To point out that they should be does nothing useful. The law has a clear role as a symbol, but symbols neither pay the bills nor shovel snow. Prohibition remains the best example of massive noncompliance in constitutional terms in our history (if you ignore the cumulative failure of the Thirteenth, Fourteenth, and Fifteenth Amendments to give Blacks actual freedom and equality). Compliance cannot be taken for granted by the government. And it cannot be forced. Only so many people can be jailed. Only so many fines can be collected. To ignore the reality of the problems of legitimacy and compliance is to dwell in a universe of verbal symbols without any awareness of the real world.

The summation of all these assertions is that the American Constitution is essentially what Aristotle thought a constitution was: a political report of the human actions and instrumentalities that encompass the whole political life of a community. The current Constitution includes, effectively, only those elements which the people of the United States and their agents will sustain. If, for example, intolerance increases over a period of time, the guarantees of the Constitution, however clearly they are stated in the document, will not protect unpopular minorities who hope for shelter under its provisions. Changes in the multitudinous aspects of the world are reflected in the current balance of power in the real Constitution. The function of the constitutional document is to define and state the relationship between the people of the United States and the various governing bodies through which those people speak.

If the people turn away from the moral and political values which guided and formed the original constitutional structure, the actual Constitution will come to reflect that corruption and will cease to be a bulwark against tyranny. No one has stated this point better than William Penn:

> But, lastly, when all is said, there is hardly one frame of government in the world so ill designed by its first founders, that, in good hands, would not do well enough. . . . Governments, like clocks, go from the motion men give them; and as governments are made and moved by men, so by them are they ruined too. Wherefore governments rather depend upon men, than men upon governments. Let men be good, and the government cannot be bad; if it be ill, they will cure it. But if men be bad, let the government be never so good, they endeavour to warp and spoil it to their turn.[18]

Before moving on, we might recapitulate the arguments about change and the Constitution. Change is inevitable, and regardless of the "model" of social and legal reality you embrace, the problem of change is crucial. The Constitution has proven to be remarkably flexible over the years—more flexible, indeed, than the framers ever dreamed. It has been said that this flexibility has come because the Constitution is what the Supreme Court justices say it is. But in the most realistic sense the Constitution is what the people say it is, and what they will sustain it to be. No conspiracy can sever the threads of the constitutional fabric, because the fabric itself is nothing more and nothing less than the composite of the people whose political community is defined and described by that Constitution.

There is no question that the existence of the written constitution and the beliefs men share about it shape actual political behavior. But it is equally obvious that actual political experience shapes men's beliefs about the written constitution. The relationship is synergistic. When various elements in the social, economic, technological, moral, and environmental fabric change, we can be sure that the results of that change will make themselves felt in the political sphere. It is less a question of causation than one of linkage. We just do not understand enough about the interrelationships and operations of society to know, much less predict, the impact and effects such changes will have. We can recognize some cause-and-effect relationships in earlier societies (however much our view is shaped by our present intellectual models), and surely this recognition can tell us that such relationships exist in our own, in areas and between elements we do not suspect.

III

The Equal Rights Amendment (ERA) has stirred more controversy than any potential constitutional alteration in the past half century. We shall examine the impulse to add the ERA to the constitutional document on rather narrow grounds. Our examination will *not* touch on "women's rights," but only on the attempt to add an amendment to the Constitution. The ERA will be our subject simply because it is very immediate. Any other ideological or programmatic amendment proposal could be substituted—"Right-to-Life," "Anti-bussing," and so on.

It has become the fashion of our time to suggest a constitutional amendment every time a political decision goes against some special interest. The number of proposals to amend the Constitution introduced on the floor of Congress each year is limited only by the number of congressmen who view such rhetorical exercises as politically valuable. In recent years that limit has not been overly restrictive. The past few years have witnessed a great increase in amendatory suggestions that are motivated less by some political problem which has plagued the constitutional system over time, such as the problems addressed by the Twenty-fifth Amendment on presidential disability and succession, than by the dictates of an ideological cause. Of course, such proposals are not new. Prohibition was the first to succeed, and few will deny that the consequences were disastrous. More recently we have added the two-term limitation on the president. The fallacy inherent in this amendment is clear. If popular election is a vital check on public officials, how is the political responsiveness of the president going to be increased by removing the check of potential reelection? The same basic argument applies to the occasionally proposed six-year single term for the chief executive.[19]

The major problem with the ERA is that it seeks to compel change in the political system in a way that is, paradoxically, both ineffective and dangerous. This can be seen by examining four major points: ideology, compliance, attitude toward the method of change, and potential impact.

There are two problems with the ideological aspect of the ERA. It appears to be grounded in an all-pervasive egalitarianism which has passed beyond attacks on overt discrimination to an assault on any form of distinction, valid or invalid. Thus, many of the very important truths which are too often discredited by the label of "Women's Lib" have very little to do with the amendatory effort on behalf of the ERA.

Another aspect of the ideological character of the ERA involves its status as a symbol. Even its most ardent supporters admit that the amendment is primarily a symbolic gesture. While agreement is not universal, there is language in the constitutional document as well as in various laws currently on the books which would accomplish the same results if compliance could be obtained. While the Constitution is replete with symbols, it is not well suited to be a dartboard for every group with a political grievance, real or imagined.

When a comparison is made between the ERA and the Child Labor Amendment in terms of the kinds of political action which have accompanied its advance, a striking difference emerges.[20] The movement against child labor only became a matter of amendment politics when all other forms of political action had been exhausted. Congress tried twice to eliminate the blight of child labor from the national economy, only to have a reactionary Supreme Court block the attempts. The dissents by Justice Holmes in *Hammer* v. *Dagenhart*[21] and Chief Justice Taft in *Bailey* v. *Drexel Furniture*[22] make it quite clear on which side ideology was rampant. It was clearly not the children's hour.

The basic difficulty with the ERA lies in the realm of compliance. It is probably true that if the same energy and dedication which has been spent on ERA had gone into seeking enforcement of laws already on the books, far more substantive progress in women's rights would have occurred. Shortly after the defeat of state Equal Rights Amendments in New York and New Jersey in 1975, a perceptive statement was made by a (woman) reporter:

> And to the other side, to the young women weeping into their discarded ERA T-shirts, one might say: cheer up, you really haven't lost anything, except time and energy that might have been better spent. Passage of ERA would not have tempered the hostility of male chauvinists; nor produced the day care centers desperately needed by working mothers; nor eased the lot of the elderly, a majority of whom happen to be women; nor helped elect more able women to major offices. So, please, let's forget the symbols and slogans and get on with the job.[23]

Recent works on compliance[24] show that even the comparatively mild step of passing a law seldom accomplishes what was intended. The element that is crucial for success in every situation is solid legal footwork. The employers who ignore the laws currently on the books are going to ignore a constitutional amendment as well until a massive amount of legal pressure is brought to bear on them. An ERA would not be self-enforcing, nor would the follow-up legislation be easy to procure. It is far easier to get votes in Congress for symbolic actions than for detailed proposals which infringe on the prerogatives of well-established groups.

Those who have worked long and hard to get the ERA passed and then ratified may easily have been taken in by a simplistic view of the process of change. The rhetoric of the movement has been clearly dependent upon the mechanistic model of change. It is assumed by the backers that the desired changes will come about by changing the words in the document itself. Somehow the words themselves are seen as performing some real and immediate action in the actual political universe. That is also the premise of magic; and even though law and magic are cognate disciplines in this respect, the effectual consequences are seldom impressive.

A telling argument against the expected success of the ERA grows out of the distinctions made earlier between the constitutional document, institutions, and culture. This division is based on the third model also discussed above.[25] The advocates of the ERA seek to alter the document when what is required by the nature of the change they seek is a change in the constitutional culture. In order to change the constitutional culture it becomes necessary to change the beliefs and practices of the population at large concerning women's rights. If this were done, the change would then permeate the constitutional institutions and probably would require no formal alteration of the central document.

> The cultural model requires [the advocates of the ERA] to shift their objective from attempts to redesign the structure and functioning of political and other institutions to the even broader task of replacing in part the substantive content of the values consensually shared by the community.[26]

Of course this is very difficult. But without the cultural change, formal changes nearly always become disfunctional: they do not accomplish what was intended.

Finally, it is not suggested that a change in the words of the constitutional document would have little or no effect. If it were to be ratified, it would begin to have impact on the surrounding institutions and culture. But, as has been stated, since the impetus behind it ignores a very basic political reality, the change would take its own path. This effect can already be seen in states which have adopted their own ERAs. The effective change required must be built on a solid cultural and institutional basis. The attempt to short-circuit the process will not succeed.[27]

IV

Those who designate one particular historical period as the time when *the* Constitution existed have serious difficulties explaining political and social change. When the complexities of incessant change are pressed on them, they usually reject the suggestion that they should be so factually intimidated. All of us, of course, are potential retrospective constitutionalists. As we confront the changes which seem to engulf us, we yearn for simpler times and less complex problems.

A major way we have dealt with the consequences of change in the United States is to refer sensitive political questions to the Supreme Court, a group whose bias, because of the nature of their background and trade, is toward the mechanistic model of constitutions and change. When the Court announces its decision it appears that a real change has taken place in the universe. But actually, no such thing has happened. While the verbal statement is effective in the legal universe, it does not always carry power into the everyday world of politics to the same extent. If a state has spent twenty-five millions in taxpayers' dollars on a project which turns out, in retrospect, to have been unconstitutional, the money doesn't magically flow back into the state treasury. And the multiplier consequences of the spending do not magically erase themselves from the homes of salaried employees who have been paid with those funds. In short, the Court's decision, however wise or unwise, adds another set of factors to the unceasing synergism of political change. Sadly, many restrospective constitutionalists cannot abide such untidiness. Their opinions and beliefs are such that without them the world becomes unendurable, and they reject reality for the comforts of the imagined past.

This method of adapting to change is time-honored in our system. But since it draws on the least realistic of the models suggested earlier, it presents a misleading picture of just how change takes place. It makes it seem far more simple than it is. And it entices groups to undertake attempts for change the wrong way.

In the face of constant change the most effective way to maintain and support the constitutional and moral norms which we hold to be necessary for our continued freedom and safety is not to withdraw from the society, cursing its failure. This Jonah-like stance is not open to us. An active attempt must be made to preserve *in the constitutional culture* those elements which will preserve the standards and principles important to us. A concentration on mechanical change in the constitutional document is misplaced. It is, after all, the behavior and inner controls of men which ultimately determine the success of a society. Imposed solutions are seldom long-range solutions. They usually become telling evidence of failure at more basic levels.

The values and principles crucial to democratic society must be alive in the minds and hearts of the people rather than just being inscribed in a few documents of awesome historicity. The Constitution is basically reflexive. It returns to the people just what the people are willing to contribute. A document cannot preserve the virtue of a polity. It can only preserve the memory of that virtue.

---

1. Only one of these constitutions has survived, and it was not discovered until comparatively recent times (see *Aristotle's Constitution of Athens and Related Texts* (n.p.: Hafner Publishing Company, 1950).

2. Glendon Schubert, *Human Jurisprudence: Public Law as Political Science* (Honolulu: The University Press of Hawaii, 1975), p. 292.

3. On this point the references could be endless. For brevity, however, see Karl Deutsch, "Mechanism, Organism, and Society: Some Models in Natural and Social Science," *Philosophy of Science* 18 (1951):230–52; and Karl Deutsch, *The Nerves of Government* (New York: The Free Press, 1963).

4. Schubert, *Human Jurisprudence*, p. 294.

5. The implications of this model are brilliantly developed by Arthur O. Lovejoy, *Reflections on Human Nature* (Baltimore, Md.: The Johns Hopkins University Press, 1961), see especially lecture 2.

6. Deutsch, *Nerves of Government*, is the seminal work in this new approach.

7. The author finds much of this approach less of a full-fledged model than the other two. The amount of jargon it uses is formidable, but it does produce insights which are valuable.

8. For some interesting reflections on this subject, see Daniel P. Moynihan, " 'Peace'—Some Thoughts on the 1960's and 1970's," *The Public Interest* 32 (Summer 1973):3–12. For a more specific work on the impact of demographic change, the following work is an analysis of the 1970 census data in terms of political impact: Joseph J. Spengler, *Population and America's Future* (San Francisco: W. H. Freeman and Company, 1975).

9. A recent example of this integrative approach is James A. Henretta, *The Evolution of American Society, 1700–1815: An Interdisciplinary Analysis* (Lexington, Mass.: D. C. Heath and Co., 1975). A massive work, using a comprehensive approach, which characterizes the "French School" is Fernand Braudel, *The Mediterranean and the Mediterranean World in the Age of Philip II*, trans. Sian Reynolds (New York: Harper and Row, 1975).

10. The best account of the Constitutional Convention is Clinton Rossiter, *1787: The Grand Convention* (New York: Macmillan Company, 1966), see especially ch. 12, 13.

11. Martin Shapiro, ed., *The Constitutional Convention: The Constitution of the United States* (New York: Appleton-Century-Crofts, 1966), pp. xxii, xxiii.

12. Elizabeth Drew, "Why Congress Won't Fight," *New York Times Magazine*, 23 September 1973.

13. Robert G. McCloskey, *The American Supreme Court* (Chicago: University of Chicago Press, 1961). See also Richard Funston, "The Supreme Court and Critical Elections," *American Political Science Review* 69(September 1975):795–811.

14. See Morton Grodzins, *The American System* (Chicago: Rand McNally, 1966). This collection of Grodzins's works on federalism is rich with insights into the structure of our system and demonstrates the impact of federalism on virtually every area of political activity.

15. See the seminal cases, *Engel v. Vitali*, 370 U.S. 421 (1962), and *Abington v. Schempp*, 374 U.S. 203 (1963). See also Richard M. Johnson, *The Dynamics of Compliance* (Evanston, Ill.: Northwestern University Press, 1967); Theodore L. Becker and Malcolm M. Feeley, *The Impact of Supreme Court Decisions*, 2nd ed. (New York: Oxford University Press, 1973); and William K. Muir, Jr., *Prayer in the Public Schools: Law and Attitude Change* (Chicago: University of Chicago Press, 1967).

16. See *Brown v. The Board of Education of Topeka, Kansas*, 347 U.S. 483 (1954); also, Richard Kluger, *Simple Justice: The History of Brown v. Board of Education and Black America's Struggle for Equality* (New York: Alfred A. Knopf, 1976); J. Peltason, *Fifty-eight Lonely Men: Southern Federal Judges and School Desegregation* (New York: Harcourt, Brace and World,

1961). The case which finally ended "massive resistance" was *Alexander* v. *Holmes County Board of Education*, 396 U.S. 19 (1969). For a consideration of the problems of northern de facto segregation, see Elanor P. Wolf, "Northern School Desegregation and Residential Choice," *1977 Supreme Court Review*, p. 63.

17. 98 U.S. 145 (1879).

18. See Daniel Boorstin, "The Perils of Indwelling Law," in *The Decline of Radicalism* (New York: Random House, 1969), p. 77.

19. Anyone who takes the trouble to read Alexander Hamilton's arguments on the question of limiting the terms a president might serve would be hard pressed to offer sufficient counter-arguments. These arguments are found in *Federalist* 72.

It is hard to maintain that the Twenty-second Amendment was anything more than a spasm (largely Republican) against the ghost of Franklin D. Roosevelt. See also George Reedy, *The Twilight of the Presidency* (New York: World Publishing Company, 1970), especially ch. 10. Another ideologically motivated amendment proposal is directed against the electoral college. The best discussion of this issue is Martin Diamond, *The Electoral College and the American Idea of Democracy* (Washington, D.C.: American Enterprise Institute, 1977).

20. See Stephen B. Wood, *Constitutional Politics in the Progressive Era* (Chicago: University of Chicago Press, 1968); and Walter I. Trattner, *Crusade for the Children* (Chicago: Quadrangle Books, 1970).

21. 247 U.S. 251 (1918).

22. 259 U.S. 20 (1922).

23. Marion K. Sanders, "Requiem for ERA," *The New Republic*, 29 November 1975, p. 21.

24. See note 15 above for the relevant works.

25. See note 2 above.

26. Schubert, *Human Jurisprudence*, p. 318.

27. A further indication of the impulse to gain their ends by short-circuiting the traditional means is the move to change the time limit on the ERA. The proponents know that there is no chance an ERA will ever get this close to ratification again, so their efforts are becoming a bit frenzied.

The Inspired Quality and the Flexibility of the Constitution *

Rex E. Lee, *professor of law and dean of the Law School at Brigham Young University, says that the Constitution is inspired but is not scripture. Professor Lee says that the inspiration is reflected in the framework of the Constitution or in its organic whole and not in its specificity. After asserting breadth and even vagueness as virtues, he proceeds to discuss briefly two areas of interest to many Mormons: the interpretation of the Constitution by the courts, and the practice of using the Constitution as an irrefutable authority. Lee's lecture is based mostly on personal experience as a practicing lawyer and as a former U.S. attorney general.*

Dean Lee is a graduate of Chicago Law School and practiced law in Phoenix, Arizona. He clerked for Justice Byron R. White at the Supreme Court and served two years as the assistant U.S. attorney general. He has argued six cases before the United States Supreme Court. In 1971 he was appointed founding dean of the J. Reuben Clark Law School at Brigham Young University.

° Adapted from "The United States Constitution: Divinity and Controversy" from *Commissioner's Lecture Series* by permission of the author and publisher; copyright 1972 by Brigham Young University Press.

WHAT DO WE MEAN when we say that the United States Constitution is inspired? Clearly the case cannot be sustained that the Constitution fits into the same category as the Book of Mormon or the Doctrine and Covenants in that every sentence and every point of doctrine are completely free from error.

Examine some of the constitutional provisions at random: members of the House of Representatives must be at least twenty-five years of age; Congress has the power to fix the standards of weights and measures; the presidential term is four years; the Supreme Court has original jurisdiction over suits involving ambassadors and appellate jurisdictions over suits between citizens of different states. It is difficult to make a very persuasive case that there is anything particularly insightful, infallible—or in some cases even good policy—about these and many other individual provisions isolated from their broader context. Indeed, there are some individual provisions that are positively offensive: the twenty-one-year constitutional protection of slavery; and the provision that in apportioning representatives and direct taxes, persons "bound to service for a term of years" count as the equivalent of three-fifths of "free persons," and that "Indians not taxed" do not count at all.

It is my opinion that the guiding hand of Deity is not reflected in each individual provision of the Constitution. I believe that some of the individual provisions were divinely inspired—those that guarantee against governmental infringement on individual liberties. But on a far grander scale, an appreciation of the divine guiding hand can be captured by focusing on the Constitution as an entirety; it is the grand view more than the micro view that must be taken. The "Miracle at Philadelphia," to use Catherine Drinker Bowen's term, was not the adoption of the commerce clause, or the lifetime appointment of judges, or the electoral college. It was the fact that the Constitution was adopted as an *entire organic* document, the fact that the delegates to the convention, representing as they did such divergent interests and possessed of such disparate philosophies, were able to reconcile their differences and to achieve the compromises characteristic of the document.

Most of the controlling constitutional concepts—separation of powers, federalism, written prohibitions against governmental intrusion on individual liberties, and, in my opinion, judicial review—are not confined to individual provisions. They pervade the entire document. Inspiration is reflected in the constitutional framework, in the total concept and overall structure, but not necessarily in each individual piece of building material.

The inspiration under which Joseph Smith translated the Book of Mormon through the Urim and Thummim was of a different quality and produced a different product than the inspiration which prevailed at the Philadelphia convention of 1787. George Washington was not a prophet, and the Constitution is not scripture.

Probably the most remarkable single aspect of the United States Constitution is that it has continued to serve as our controlling organic document through almost two centuries of the most far-reaching political, social, and economic change that any nation has ever experienced. The amendments do not provide the reason. With the exception of the first ten amendments—which for historic purposes must be included as part of the original document—the post-Civil War amendments are the only ones whose doctrinal importance ranks with the provisions of the original Constitution.

How, then, is it possible that the same basic set of governmental powers and limitations could suffice for one hundred eighty-nine years of such explosive growth? The answer is found in the breadth—or if you will, the vagueness—of the most important constitutional principles. For unlike the approach taken to many state constitutions, our Founding Fathers did not attempt to prescribe with detail the governmental powers and prohibitions contained in our national Constitution. They set the general course for the new ship of state, but left the helmsmen ample navigational freedom.

The resulting breadth and flexibility are the chief reasons that the Constitution has remained our most durable single source of law—and indeed the underlying basis for most of our law—throughout almost two centuries of overwhelming change. I believe that eighteen decades of intervening history have borne out the wisdom of this broad-brush approach. I also submit that the grand constitutional design of breadth rather than specificity is additional evidence of divine influence.

But the breadth and vagueness of the leading provisions of our national Constitution are not an unmixed blessing. Just as they are the foundation stone of constitutional durability, they have also been the source of controversy. I would like to explore two such controversies. The first concerns the power which judges exercise in interpreting the Constitution. The second pertains to the use of the Constitution as an irrefutable authority.

I
Interpretation or Legislation

A frequent criticism directed against American courts, and particularly against the United States Supreme Court, is that the judges have usurped the role of the legislators. The argument is that they are not interpreting the Constitution but rather legislating *pursuant to it,* or even worse, attempting to rewrite it.

One of my favorite stories came from a Supreme Court justice. A friend of his had commented concerning the advisability of a constitutional convention: "Well, I can tell you one thing, it would be better than those unauthorized constitutional conventions you guys hold every Friday" (referring to the Court's Friday conferences at which the justices vote on pending cases).

There is merit in some criticism of the Court for stepping over the boundary between judicial interpretation and legislative lawmaking. But much of the criticism is based upon a lack of understanding of the document itself. The key to understanding is the breadth of the document and its accompanying vagueness, referred to earlier. Consider some of the important constitutional provisions:

1. "The Congress shall have Power . . . to regulate Commerce with foreign Nations, and among the several States, and with the Indian Tribes . . ." (Art. 1, sec. 8).

2. "Full Faith and Credit shall be given in each State to the public Acts, Records, and judicial Proceedings of every other State" (Art. 4, sec. 1).

3. "The Congress shall have Power to lay and collect Taxes, Duties, Imposts and Excises, to pay the Debts and provide for the common Defence and general Welfare of the United States . . ." (Art. 1, sec. 8).

4. "Congress shall make no law respecting an establishment of religion, or prohibiting the free exercise thereof; or abridging the freedom of speech, or of the press; or the right of the public peaceably to assemble, and to petition the government for a redress of grievances" (Amend. 1).

5. "No State shall . . . deprive any person of life, liberty, or property, without due process of law . . ." (Amend. 14, sec. 1).

6. "No State shall . . . deny to any person within its jurisdiction the equal protection of the laws" (Amend. 14, sec. 1).

These are some of the most important provisions of the United States Constitution. Yet I defy anyone to give me the "plain meaning" of these provisions in all aspects of their potential application. Is it constitutional for state governments to supply free textbooks to church-sponsored primary schools? Or how about state grants for the construction of parochial school buildings? Or free bus service? Or paying a portion of teachers' salaries? The only prohibition contained in the Constitution is against the "establishment of religion." These and many other questions are simply not reached by the "plain meaning" of the phrase "establishment of religion."

Similarly, the prohibition against denial of "equal protection of the laws" on its face provides very little guidance on such issues as whether state-provided facilities—buses, waiting rooms, schools, beaches, playgrounds, or anything else—which are equal in quality but separately maintained on the basis of race satisfy the constitutional mandate: "equal protection of laws."

One of the fascinating aspects of Mr. Justice Black's approach to constitutional litigation is his belief that constitutional provisions on their face provide clear guides for judicial decisions. During a television interview a few years ago, a reporter attempted to engage the Justice in a discussion of *Miranda* v. *Arizona*, 384 U.S. 436 (1966). That decision held inadmissible in a criminal trial the confession of the accused taken in the absence of careful and detailed warnings concerning his constitutional rights. Mr. Justice Black's response was as refreshing as it was amazing. He simply pulled out his little paperback edition of the Constitution, thumbed through it until he came to the Fifth Amendment, and responded, as best as I remember: "It says right here, 'No person . . . shall be compelled in any criminal case to be a witness against himself, nor be deprived of life, liberty, or property, without due process of law.' " In Mr. Justice Black's view, the correctness of the *Miranda* holding, as well as its detailed formula, were spelled out in good plain English in the Constitution's privilege against self-incrimination and "due process of law" provisions. On another occasion, he made a similar statement about the Court's earlier holding *Wickard* v. *Filburn*, 317 U.S. 111 (1942). In that case the Court held that a farmer growing wheat in Ohio and using it to feed his livestock on his farm was engaged in "interstate commerce" notwithstanding the fact that the grain never left the farmer's premises. In Justice Black's opinion, it was all right there in the Constitution for anyone to read.

The point is not the correctness or incorrectness of *Miranda* v. *Arizona* or *Wickard* v. *Filburn*. The point is that these issues cannot be resolved on the basis of the "plain meaning" of the Constitution. The same is true of the overwhelming majority of important constitutional decisions which the Court has handed down during the some one hundred seventy years since

Marbury v. *Madison*, 1 Cranch 137, 2 L. Ed. 60 (1803). With all due deference to Mr. Justice Black, our Constitution simply does not permit resolution of constitutional issues by flipping to the appropriate page and declaring, "Here is the answer."

The starting point for analysis is the extraordinary breadth of the most important constitutional provisions. Some governmental entity must be given the authority to impart meaning to such terms by interpreting them. In 1803 the Supreme Court held in *Marbury* v. *Madison* that the interpretative responsibility was intended to be vested in the courts. The Constitution itself is silent on the subject. If we accept the correctness of *Marbury*, then it necessarily follows that the continuing task of pouring content into such expansive terms as "freedom of religion," "regulation of interstate commerce," "equal protection," and "due process of law" was to be vested in the courts, and discharged by them as they decided actual cases and controversies, on a case-to-case basis. Each of their decisions then gave further meaning to the general concepts of the Constitution, making incremental additions to the growing body of constitutional law.

To those who find such judicial power offensive, I have several observations.

The notion that judges are solely interpreters of the law and never the sources of the law is out of harmony with the theoretical underpinnings of the common law inherited from England and prevailing in this country since the first settlers landed in Jamestown. Throughout the eight centuries of its existence, the distinctive characteristic of the common law—and the chief source of its genius—has been the authority of the judges to exercise lawmaking power, at least within a limited sphere. It also seems clear from my reading of the Constitution and its history that the continuing existence of the common law was a fundamental underlying assumption of the Constitution makers.

Do judges make constitutional law and formulate constitutional policy? Of course they do. Given constitutional vagueness, they would find it impossible to perform their obligation to decide cases and controversies without making constitutional law. Those who are offended must lay most of the blame—or credit—at the doorstep of the Constitution makers.

But to the equally important question "Do judges sometimes overstep their bounds in making policy?" the answer is equally clear: *yes*. And here lies the dilemma that inevitably accompanies constitutional breadth and the power of judicial review. Necessarily wrapped up in the same package with constitutional flexibility and durability is the potential for judicial abuse. Is there any possible check against such abuse? I believe that the only really effective check is an attitude of cautious restraint imposed by the judges upon themselves. One alternative would be to adopt a constitution characterized by lesser breadth than the provisions of our own inspired Constitution. That is not a realistic alternative for a nation as dynamic as ours because of the sacrifice in flexibility. The first line of defense against judicial overreaching, therefore, must be in the judges. The concomitant of judicial power is not judicial overreaching, but judicial restraint.

Basic choices between competing policy considerations should be upset only if they contravene constitutional provisions. The breadth of our Constitution gives the judges substantial elbow room, but nowhere are they given the authority to go beyond the prescriptions contained within the four corners of the Constitution. The dividing line between constitutional adjudication and judicial legislation is sometimes difficult to identify, but its conceptual existence and the need to strive perpetually for its identification and respect should be ever-present judicial imperatives.

It is said that the courts are the final authority on issues of constitutionality, and in a sense this is true. But in a broader sense, the final source of constitutional authority is the American people. Even though members of our federal judiciary are appointed for life, I believe there is a long-term response between the broadly held views of the American people and the decisions of our federal courts. This long-range interaction between the people and the courts was exemplified by Richard Nixon's 1968 campaign promise to appoint "strict constructionists" to the Supreme Court.

May I say parenthetically that I cannot think of a more inappropriate description of a Supreme Court justice than the phrase "strict constructionist." The term has its own built-in refutation. Strict construction of the United States Constitution is an impossibility because it is not a strict document. I suspect that Richard Nixon, who is a good lawyer, really knew this. But though a good lawyer, he is an even better politician; and for all of its analytical drawbacks, "strict construction" is a catchy phrase with political appeal. It has another political attraction. It is capable of connoting whatever image the speaker—or even more important, the listener—wants it to connote.

I suspect that what Mr. Nixon was really saying, or at least what most people—including me—interpreted him to be saying, was that he was unhappy with the direction the Court's decisions were taking—particularly in criminal decisions. He intended to appoint justices whose views might alter the Court's direction. This experience from 1968 to the present illustrates that our Constitution does make the judiciary responsive to the will of the people.

Nixon's promises concerning Supreme Court appointments were a major component of his 1968 campaign. I believe that this aspect of his campaign appealed to many people. He was elected president and appointed four new justices who have substantially altered the direction and content of the Court's decisions. Not as immediately and directly responsive as in the case of the president, the Congress was responsive, over the long run. And in matters of constitutional adjudication—the principal calling of our federal court system—it is the long run that counts.

II
Irrefutable Authority

There is a second aspect of constitutional breadth that I would like to discuss. I believe that lack of precision renders any authoritative document a handy weapon that can be drafted into service for a variety of purposes. It can be used on either side of an argument and indeed on both sides at the same time.

I think that the most potent of all weapons in the winning of arguments is the irrefutable authority. If you can press into service an authority of unquestioned and unquestionable stature, then the argument necessarily comes to an end, and you have won.

The most potent choice of irrefutable authority is scripture. God himself is the only infallible source of knowledge and truth upon which we can rely without question and without qualification. Not far behind the scriptures in the hierarchy of irrefutable authority is the United States Constitution, for two very good reasons. In the first place, it is the only document, so far as I know, which came from a source other than a prophet of the Lord but which nevertheless has been given at least a measure of scriptural approval. Since the scriptural approval is sometimes misunderstood, as discussed earlier, the tendency may exist to place the Constitution on the same level with scripture itself. Secondly, the Constitution is the supreme law of the land, the most important single source of American law, and the foundation upon which other sources rest.

I have no criticism of the basic concept of irrefutable authority. Properly employed, it is the easiest, the surest, and the proper way to resolve conflicts. There is an omnipresent temptation, however, to rely on such authority regardless of its applicability; and I know of no better examples than the scriptures and the Constitution.

We find it easy to lapse into the expansive notion that the Constitution, like the gospel, embraces all truth and that it protects and guarantees all that is right, equitable, and just. From that grand premise it is only a short and comfortable leap to the proposition that the Constitution embraces *my* particular notion of what is right, equitable, and just. The Constitution lends itself to this kind of use because of its breadth.

Issues such as foreign aid, fluoridation of water, public versus private education, progressive income tax, to which political party I should belong and which candidate I should support; questions about economic development and environmental quality control; questions about the power of labor unions and the influence of big business in government—all these are issues of great importance. But these questions cannot and ought not to be resolved by simply resorting to irrefutable authority. Neither the Constitution nor the scriptures contain answers to these questions, and under the grand plan of eternal progress it is our responsibility to develop our own skills by working out our own answers through our own thought processes.

For example, the Constitution authorizes an income tax, but it neither commands nor forbids an income tax. That is a policy issue on which the Constitution—and the scriptures—are silent. Attempting to resolve our differences of opinion by asserting that if our opponents only understood the scriptures or the Constitution they would see that the whole answer is contained therein only results in foreclosing the careful, rational attention that these issues deserve and require. Resorting to several broad provisions of the Constitution in answer to that kind of question is just plain intellectual laziness.

We, of all people, have an obligation to respect the Constitution—to respect it not only for what it is and what it does, but also for what it is *not* and what it does *not* do. For in this as in other contexts, improper use of that which is grand can only result in the diminution of its grandeur.

Conclusion

In most legal documents imprecision, breadth, and vagueness are characteristics to be avoided. Yet these are *the* distinctive characteristics of the United States Constitution. As is the case with indefinite language in any setting, the breadth of our Constitution imposes significant costs. Chief among these costs are lack of predictability, and necessary policy-making authority in the federal judges who are charged with the responsibility of pouring content into such phrases as "free exercise of religion" and "equal protection of the laws."

I believe that these costs are worth paying. If the Founding Fathers had attempted to go beyond the prescription of broad generalities in such important areas as the Bill of Rights and the exclusivity of Congress's authority over interstate commerce, the Constitution could not have survived change of the unforeseen and unforeseeable magnitude that our nation has experienced since 1789. For these reasons I believe that the breadth of our Constitution is one aspect in which divine influence is manifest.

Some Thoughts about our Constitution and Government

Neal A. Maxwell, a General Authority of The Church of Jesus Christ of Latter-day Saints, makes some important observations about our constitutional system and our responsibilities as citizens. In his lecture he says that man hungers for freedom but also he seeks order. But, he asks, has man become more concerned with order and his personal welfare than with the liberty of others? Are we the same champions of agency we were in the pre-existence? Can we meet the challenges of those "just and holy principles" found in the U.S. Constitution? Elder Maxwell talks about the need to be informed, and he says that if we are "to bring to pass much righteousness" we must be righteous. We must be, as Professors Reynolds and Bushman assert, men of virtue if the American constitutional system is to endure. On the question of government, Elder Maxwell turns to the warnings of both ancient and modern prophets who have spoken on the matter, and he enjoins the Latter-day Saints to respond to these warnings and to meet their responsibilities as citizens.

Elder Maxwell took a graduate degree in political science and has served in government and in higher education. He has taught American political thought and has served as vice-president of the University of Utah. While serving as Commissioner of Education for The Church of Jesus Christ of Latter-day Saints he was called to be a General Authority, and he is currently one of the presidents of the First Quorum of the Seventy.

IN THE PREMORTAL WORLD we agreed to submit ourselves to a moral frame of reference which would place a heavy emphasis on freedom, with *all* the risks that freedom entails. In his own way William James surmises:

> Suppose that the world's author put the case to you before creation, saying: "I am going to make a world not certain to be saved, a world the perfection of which shall be conditional merely, the condition being that each several agent does his own level best." I offer you the chance of taking part in such a world. Its safety, you see, is unwarranted. It is a real adventure, with real danger, yet it may win through. . . . Will you trust yourself and trust the other agents to face the risk?[1]

In the premortal councils, we understand, many rejected the proffered world with agency and risk. That rejection foreshadowed the fundamental nature of man's freedom and free ambivalence toward agency. Man hungers for freedom and liberty, but he also needs and seeks order and security. Filling *both* cravings is difficult. Will and Ariel Durant highlight the dilemma well when they state that "when liberty destroys order, the hunger for order will destroy liberty."[2]

It is obvious that in his pursuit of order and security, man often compromises the very agency over which the war in heaven was fought. Agency is used to reject agency and to reject the load of liberty and the consequences of continual choices. Remember, Jesus had a great following, until he began to preach certain terrifying truths. "Many of his disciples went back, and walked no more with him" (John 6:66).

But the hunger for order is not the only human impulse that destroys agency. Remember, too, that in the premortal world Lucifer was more concerned with his own ascendancy than with the agency of others. In this world, many of us are more concerned with our own worldly status or welfare than with the liberty of others.

We may have been "for" agency then, but are we now? Life's challenges are stern, and most of us are inconsistent and uneven in our devotion to liberty.

A gospel understanding of the premortal circumstances is crucial indeed! It can help us to meet the challenges posed by life. As Nancy Newhall wrote:

> . . . Not dulled, nor lulled, supine, secure, replete, does man create; But out of stern challenge . . . From what immortal desire . . . surges that desire? What flint of fact . . . or far horizon, ignites that spark? What cry, what music, what strange beauty, strikes that resonance? On these hangs the future of the world.[3]

Knowledge of the premortal circumstances and decisions is the "flint of fact" that can spark our resolve to govern ourselves politically in a setting of liberty.

Our American Constitution places heavy duties on the individual citizen—just as the gospel does. The Constitution depends on a sufficient number of strong citizens for its very establishment; it will depend, likewise, on a crucial mass of strong and able citizens for its preservation. Thus, that the Constitution will one day be "upon the brink of ruin" and on "the very verge of destruction"[4] should not surprise us. Societies composed of strong citizens willing and able to maintain freedom and to cope with its frustrations are not common. Consider, for instance, those situations such as obtained in Sodom which were self-terminating: a doomed people who because of their unrighteousness simply became extinct, save for three survivors.

Or again, consider the examples in the Book of Mormon where earlier disciples of Christ produced periodic cultural and spiritual excellence but soon were overcome by the world in a rhythm of rising and falling. Or think of the "Dunkirks" in which God's people have been driven and dislodged but emerged elsewhere intact—as did ancient Israel and the Latter-day Saints in this dispensation.

Consider the poignancy of Pilate yielding to the mob rather than to justice and truth. The Pilates and Agrippas of the world, in a sense, are among the most tragic of human figures. One senses that at times they really are persuaded, but are not willing to counter prevailing opinion and respond to the truth because the political price is too high.

We, like Pilate and Agrippa, often face the challenge of countering the prevailing opinion. Our calling in this time is to establish latter-day Zions in the midst of a world that is growing more wicked, more careless, and more standardless as to spiritual things. In this interactive setting we will share many of the problems of our fellowmen. Given the difficulty of our calling and the sometimes hostile conditions of our environment, what and how shall we do? We would do best to follow the prophet! He, under God's direction, will lead in those moments when we must "bear it patiently" (D&C 98:23). He will help us to be able to see, when in our anxiety we need to, those things that will be our reassuring equivalent of what Elisha's young friend saw: "horses and chariots of fire"! (2 Kings 6:17).

What follow are some less important observations and suggestions for which I pretend no sanction except my own.

Thomas Jefferson was right when he observed that the future of our republic would depend on its citizens' being attentive and informed. This, in turn, will require a strong commitment to the First Amendment so far as the dispensing of information, values, and ideas is concerned. We have a great stake in all the American constitutional principles, but some are apt to prove more crucial than others, such as the First Amendment. Benjamin Franklin knew much about the ecology of freedom, for as early as 1722 he said:

> This sacred Privilege is so essential to free Governments, that the Security of Property, and the Freedom of Speech always go together; and in those wretched Countries where a Man cannot call his Tongue his own, he can scarce call any Thing else his own. Whoever would overthrow the Liberty of a Nation, must begin by subduing the Freeness of Speech.[5]

But even the powerful First Amendment is no guarantee against apathy. Indeed, according to the research of Seymour Marvin Lipset, apathy appears to be one of the unintended by-products of democracy. Apathy companies with affluence and ennui.

Juxtaposed with apathy is the challenge of hyperactivism—which is so often narrow and strident. Samuel P. Huntington sagely writes:

> The vulnerability of democratic government in the United States thus comes not primarily from external threats, though such threats are real . . . but from the internal dynamics of democracy itself in a highly educated, mobilized, and participant society. "Democracy never lasts long," John Adams observed. "It soon wastes, exhausts, and murders itself. There never was a democracy yet that did not commit suicide." That suicide is more likely to be the product of overindulgence than of any other cause.[6]

Perhaps in no realm is the challenge to Latter-day Saints to contribute productively to our nation more real than in the realms of community life and government at all levels. We should do our duty and be attentive and informed. We surely need the gift of the Holy Ghost to select "good causes" and to take inspired initiatives. We are reminded that the power is in us to do much good and to "bring to pass much righteousness." (See D&C 58:26-28.)

Presumably, the causes we select will be consistent with "just and holy principles" (D&C 101:77) and with "that law of the land which is constitutional" (D&C 98:6). Those are rigorous criteria—not the kind of criteria designed to launch us on personal ego trips or on unsound crusades!

Inspired idealism and wise activism are needed today. There are many who are filled with Martha-like anxiety about America, but in order to be truly helpful our actions should be tested by these criteria. As Church members we have counsel concerning this challenge of citizenship in a 1968 First Presidency statement, which I quote in full:

> The First Presidency wish to bring to the attention of the members of the Church of Jesus Christ of Latter-day Saints their obligations as members of the communities in which they live and as citizens of the nation.
>
> The historic position of the Church has been one which is concerned with the quality of man's contemporary environment as well as preparing him for eternity. In fact, as social and political conditions affect man's behavior now, they obviously affect eternity.
>
> The revelations in this dispensation place a sobering responsibility on us as individuals in seeking out and supporting political candidates who are "wise," "good," and "honest." Likewise, the health of our cities and communities is as genuine a concern now as it was in the planning and establishment of Nauvoo or Salt Lake City.
>
> The growing world-wide responsibilities of the Church make it inadvisable for the Church to seek to respond to all the various and complex issues involved in the mounting problems of the many cities and communities in which members live. But this complexity does not absolve members as individuals from filling their responsibilities as citizens in their own communities.
>
> We urge our members to do their civic duty and to assume their responsibilities as individual citizens in seeking solutions to the problems which beset our cities and communities.
>
> With our wide ranging mission, so far as mankind is concerned, Church members cannot ignore the many practical problems that require solution if our families are to live in an environment conducive to spirituality.
>
> Where solutions to these practical problems require cooperative action with those not of our faith, members should not be reticent in doing their part in joining and leading in those efforts where they can make an individual contribution to those causes which are consistent with the standards of the Church.
>
> Individual Church members cannot, of course, represent or commit the Church, but should, nevertheless, be "anxiously engaged" in good causes, using the principles of the Gospel of Jesus Christ as their constant guide.[7]

Incidentally, this First Presidency statement was used again recently by Elder Ezra Taft Benson, President of the Council of the Twelve, in a statement concerning the challenges of maintaining domestic tranquility in the United States of America.[8]

As Latter-day Saints we do not have the option Jonah thought he had—that of declaring the impending destruction of Nineveh and then waiting as an observer on the hillside to view the cataclysm. It is exceedingly important that Latter-day Saints avoid both the "bunker" and the "onlooker" mentalities.

Latter-day Saints, for instance, carry the burden and responsibility of seeking out wise, good, and honest political leaders, which does not mean merely waiting for others to create candidate options and then complaining about those options. How much needless human misery has been caused by leaders who have been bright but bad, clever but dishonest, or good but naive and unwise. The selection of qualified leaders, then, should be an enterprise of paramount importance to all Latter-day Saints.

Thus, quality of life depends upon the quality of both the leaders and the people as well as upon the form of government. The word *civilization* is used only twice in the Book of Mormon (Alma 51:22 and Moroni 9:11). It is impressive to note (Moroni 9) that the loss of civilization was tied to the growing immorality, not to a decline in Nephite art, though art no doubt declined, too. The growing anarchy was a reflection of a decline in their capacity to love God and their fellowmen, not a decline in their architecture, though the latter no doubt reflected decay too. The author who chronicled this earlier American society commented on his people's perversion and violence, not just the failure of their political systems to perform. Thus, at the very core, the inner deficiencies of man determine the outer or institutional manifestations, not the reverse! *The collapse of individuals always precedes the collapse of systems!* Thus, if we are "to bring to pass much righteousness," we must be righteous individuals. There can be no lasting civilization without creative civility. And what better gentles us than the gospel? What better encourages the creative use of our talents to help others than the gospel?

The flow of information and inspiration to and from the people and their leaders plays a significant role in the shaping of any society. Basic public opinion is a crucial but unwritten part of our inspired constitutional process.

Canadian W. L. Mackenzie King once said: "Government, in the last analysis, is organized opinion. Where there is little or no public opinion, there is likely to be bad government."[9]

The Prophet Joseph urged the Saints to be righteously influential in the contest of ideas and opinions. As Aaron Wildavsky noted recently:

Ultimately, [Lord] Bryce was convinced, "republics live by Virtue"— with a capital "V", meaning "the maintenance of a high level of public spirit and justice among the citizens." Note: "among the citizens," not merely among public officials. For how could leaders rise so far above the led; or, stemming from the people, be so superior to them; or, held accountable, stray so far from popular will? Surely it would be surprising if the vices of politicians stemmed from the virtues of the people. What the people do to their leaders must be at least as important as what the leaders do to them.[10]

I have always been reassured by King Mosiah's statement that "it is not common that the voice of the people desireth anything contrary to that which is right; but it is common for the lesser part of the people to desire that which is not right" (Mosiah 29:26). This view rests upon the assumption that the people would choose right if they had adequate information and inspiration. But information by itself does not automatically provide motivation; values provide our motivation as well as our moorings. "Why" is at least as important as "what" and "how" in the direction of human affairs.

Sometimes subverting Caesars get power through the indifference and apathy of large numbers of citizens. Other times, the "voice of the people" may be manipulated. As James Q. Wilson observed: "Today, not only does political action follow quickly upon the stimulus of public interest, but government itself creates that stimulus and sometimes acts in advance of it."[11]

To the extent that Latter-day Saints are less addicted to federal programs and handouts than other people, we are in a better position to resist caressing Caesars. Federal handouts and programs can be addicting, and addicts are not likely to reform the pusher. Obviously, there are some situations in which government help should be given to individuals—sometimes temporarily, sometimes extensively.

In the last analysis our constitutional freedoms are far more apt to be tested by the internal manipulation of smiling Caesars than by external pirates boarding the ship of state. As Wilson also stated regarding the American Revolution: "Except for the issue of taxation, which raised for the colonists major questions of representation, almost all of their complaints involved *the abuse of administrative powers.*"[12] Caesar's smile can become a grim grin, after all.

In his play *Knickerbocker Holiday,* Maxwell Anderson has one of his characters make this sardonic statement about swollen and serious government: "Since we have to have one or the other let's throw out this professional and go back to the rotation of amateurs! Let's keep the government small and funny, and maybe it'll give us less discipline and more entertainment!"[13]

Going the second citizen-mile includes not only Church service but community service as well. Latter-day Saints should remember that bureaucratic Caesarism has grown as volunteerism has ebbed.

If we think about it very long, the justifiable criticism of political leaders is not, after all, a criticism of the old-fashioned virtues but a painful declaration of their absence. When our political leaders lose their personal humility, they forget that he who would be the highest should be the servant of all. When our leaders become manipulative or corrupt, they demonstrate the searing scriptural truth: that "almost all" of us misuse power and authority (see D&C 121:39). The political leaders whom we venerate the most, such as Washington and Lincoln, generally reflect the style of leadership so beautifully set forth in section 121 of the Doctrine and Covenants.

Political leaders can be too insulated from real life, too far from the experience of the common man. We have before us the scriptural insight of King Mosiah, who labored to maintain himself rather than be supported by the people. This king was beloved because he cared about liberty and was not a tyrant. He was not enriched by public service; he was peaceful and just. King Mosiah's style is a striking contrast, is it not, to the style of Solomon? Little wonder that, for these and other reasons, the constituents of King Mosiah "did esteem him more than any other man . . . yea, exceedingly, beyond measure" (Mosiah 29:40).

Righteous people can, like Mosiah, be bold without being overbearing. They can, more often than they know, make a difference in human affairs. When for too long good men do nothing, soon nothing can be done. The Saints of God must stand in holy places. They must also stand on just and holy principles in order to be the leaven of which the Savior spoke.

Modern prophets in our time have surely not been mute. They have issued warning signals, but often these statements have been ignored. Consider the statements of the Brethren stretching over decades on the evils of the dole and the challenge of big government. Or take as an example the statement of President Clark on the importance of local government:

> Liberty will never depart from us while we have local self-government controlling and directing matters pertaining to our personal liberties and to the security of our private property; it will not abide with us if we shall lose this local self-government.[14]

Currently the Brethren have spoken out strongly on various trends, such as abortion and pornography. In general, our society's response to these warnings has been disappointing. Why?

First, there are the distractions of materialism and affluence. The apostle John, when trying to exhort one group of people, characterized their response as: "I am rich, and increased with goods, and have need of nothing" (Revelation 3:17). Life-styles which aim at pleasure and the eat-drink-and-be-merry philosophy are not new challenges to the prophets.

Second, many genuinely believe that there is really nothing new or alarming that is happening and, therefore, nothing to be concerned about. The people of Noah's time had probably seen it rain hard before.

Third, as in the past, when prophets have accurately foretold events, the reactions of cynics and skeptics was that the prophets had simply guessed right, so why listen?

Fourth, and perhaps most important, some people tend to disregard warning signals because they come from a seemingly obscure prophet of an apparently obscure Church. These signals contravene the fashionable views of the time.

The people of God must never worry about being mocked for doing what is right. After all, the pointing finger of scorn will, one day, in a spasm turn back on its owner. Better to be a Uriah briefly mocked than a smooth David suffering for years. Better to suffer a wrong than to do a wrong.

Our wise Founding Fathers clearly gave us a superbly written Constitution, but what they could not automatically pass on to succeeding generations was their courage and their commitment to the grand principles in that Constitution. These are things each generation must supply for its own time. There are even times when wise and righteous leaders are not able to persuade their own peers. You may recall the poignant prayer of Mormon, who interceded for his people but candidly observed that it was a prayer "without faith" because of their continued slackness and hardness of heart (see Mormon 3:12).

We must not assume, either, that there is any historical momentum which favors muddling through somehow. People or leaders who have become distracted from true values or who carry in their luggage of life only the neglected and eroded remains of parental values will be mauled by circumstances and situations. Political leaders who shun the standards of the centuries are apt to be lost in a desert with no stars to guide by.

What we truly believe truly matters. Creeds count; beliefs and behavior are linked. I believe that the Lord's answer to Joseph Smith's inquiry about which church to join was an answer in which the Lord clearly denounced all human value and belief systems that are not based upon the whole of truth. The Lord's answer was not simply a comment on the contending sects in northern New York, though the divine reply met the Prophet's immediate need in that respect. Human systems, even though they include some commendable things and some truth, are not acceptable to God because they are contaminated by incorrect principles which produce varying measures of mortal misery. God loves us and desires our full happiness here and complete salvation in the world to come. He recognizes our need for truth as well as liberty. Both were at issue in the premortal councils, and both are at issue here and now.

In conclusion may I share with you some lines from an address in Independence Hall, February 22, 1861, by Abraham Lincoln:

> I have often pondered over the dangers which were incurred by the men who assembled here and framed and adopted that Declaration. I have pondered over the toils that were endured by the officers and soldiers of the army, who achieved that Independence. I have often inquired of myself, what great principle or idea it was that kept this Confederacy so long together. It was not the mere matter of the separation of the colonies from the mother land; but that sentiment in the Declaration of Independence which gave *liberty, not alone to the people of this country, but hope to the world* for all future time. It was that which gave promise that in due time the weights should be lifted from the shoulders of all men, and that *all* should have an equal chance. This is the sentiment embodied in that Declaration of Independence.[15]

So much depends upon America. We are still the hope of the world, as Lincoln asserted. If we were to fail, we would fail twice—once for ourselves and once for all mankind! May God prepare us and preserve us so to serve and so to live, I pray in the name of Jesus Christ. Amen.

---

1. *Pragmatism* (New York: Longmans, Green, and Co., 1946), pp. 290–91.

2. Quoted in Virginia P. Frobes, "Living in My Father's House" (Thirty-second Annual Frederick William Reynolds Lecture, delivered at the University of Utah, 19 February 1968), p. 5.

3. "Everest: The West Ridge," *National Geographic*, October 1963, p. 30.

4. Joseph Smith, speech given 19 July 1840 (Ms d 155, Bx 4, Archives, Church Historical Department [The Church of Jesus Christ of Latter-day Saints], Salt Lake City, Utah).

5. Benjamin Franklin, *The Papers of Benjamin Franklin*, ed. Leonard W. Labaree, Whitfield J. Bell, et al. (New Haven, Conn.: Yale University Press, 1959), 1:27.

6. "The Democratic Distemper," *Public Interest* 41 (Fall 1975): 37.

7. *Deseret News*, 7 September 1968.

8. Speech given 21 October 1975 in Denver, Colorado.

9. Quoted in John Bartlett, *Familiar Quotations*, 14th ed. (Boston: Little, Brown and Co., 1968), p. 931.

10. "The Past and Future Presidency," *Public Interest* 41 (Fall 1975): 57.

11. "The Rise of the Bureaucratic State," *Public Interest* 41 (Fall 1975): 103.

12. Ibid., p. 101; italics added, except for the word *administrative*.

13. *Knickerbocker Holiday* (Washington, D.C.: Anderson House, 1938), p. 101.

14. J. Reuben Clark, Jr., "Prophecies, Penalties, and Blessings," *The Improvement Era*, July 1940, p. 443.

15. Abraham Lincoln, *The Collected Works of Abraham Lincoln*, ed. Roy P. Basler, Marion Dolores Pratt, and Lloyd A. Dunlap (New Brunswick, N.J.: Rutgers University Press, 1953), 4:240; italics added, except for the word *all*. The original copy was published in the Philadelphia *Inquirer*, but important variations as recorded in the New York *Tribune* have been honored in this quote.

Index